To Mavis.

Freddie Carpenter

Jeroy.

ACID
DROPS

CLASSIFICATION: POETRY

A CIP catalogue record for this book is available from
the British Library.

Printed and bound in Great Britain.

Paper used in the production of books published by
United Press comes only from sustainable forests.

ISBN 978-1-84436-659-0

First published in Great Britain in 2008 by
United Press Ltd
Admail 3735
London
EC1B 1JB
Tel: 0870 240 6190
Fax: 0870 240 6191
All Rights Reserved

www.unitedpress.co.uk

CONTENTS

1943

I remember that time in '43
When I was young and fancy free.
Wings on my breast and stripes on my arm,
Facing each day without a qualm,
Sharing a tent on Africa's shore.
How could a young blood ask for more.
Flying so low o'er a still blue sea,
Seeking prey where it might be.
Eager to make that killing shot,
Caring nought for my enemy's lot.
Knowing some magic, lucky charm
Would always keep me safe from harm;
Though, all too often, six flew out
But one at least was counted out.

The Sergeants' Mess was a dim-lit tent
And every night that's where we went ...
Trestle tables and a sandy floor.
Drank too much ... then drank some more.
Learned the words of age-old ditties,
Verses known in Eastern cities.
Knew every line of Eskimo Nell,
The Ball of Kerrymuir as well.
Drank to the health of Cardinal Puff.
Dared not say we'd had enough.
Just Boy Scouts in a world of men.
Growing up fast as we all did then.

Stood in line to get our pay.
Lost it by the fourteenth day,
For poker was the only game
And some old sweats made prior claim,
For they had learned to play the fool
When we were still just boys at school,
And, when we sang of Raffles Square,
They would smile for they'd been there.

Though Death was king and made his cull,
Life was lived to the very full.
And you may scoff and moralise,
But forgive me if I think otherwise.

A FISH CALLED WANDA

There's something fishy going on, I'm sure
And I'm quite convinced it's far from pure.
Clandestine meetings in the village hall,
Arcane chantings to a coven's call.
Panpipes wailing like a crazy loon
Or harpies howling to a crescent moon.?
My eye is pressed to a crack in the door.
Yet gripped by fear, I want to know more.
Though clad in Barbour, brogue and tweed,
It's clear to me they're Satan's seed.
A mezzo croons as if to a child
And Stentor roars, his eyes all wild.
Foul Hecate stands, her arms high-raised;
The souls all hers, all lost, all crazed.

What might we see when the moon is high;
Cavorting that's not for the timid or shy?
Dancing all naked in the Cotswold night ...
Arthritic limbs in the moon's pale light?
Withered paps all spent and flat,
Goose-bumped bellies running to fat.

Not a sight to gladden the eye!
"Away, foul fiends!" I want to cry.
Yet, all the same, I'd like to knowWho makes them put on
such a show,
Though, when I'm feeling liverish,
I put it all down to the price of fish.

A VILLAGE POET

When the mood's upon me, I like to write,
Reveal my thoughts in black and white.
How it was when I was small,
Lowly roots held tight in thrall.
Then stirring days when I was free
To give full rein to the inner me.
To flirt with death and play his game ...
How could life be ever the same!
And such excitement as fate could fashion
Of tropic nights and hot young passion.
Then the rural dream of peace and calm
To quiet the heart with healing balm.
So many paths in later life,
Sometimes sweetness, sometimes strife.
Words and music, all a part
Of memory sharp as Cupid's dart.

To be perfectly honest, I have to say,
I'm surprised my jingles saw light of day.
The problem for me always seems to be
That my errant pen runs away from me
I try to hold to a fairly low key ...
Then it all turns out to be rather naughtee!
My censor's patience has finally snapped;
You wouldn't believe how much I've scrapped!
But, before I was raised to a higher address,
I was a choral scholar in the Sergeants' Mess
And, when I recall some ditties I knew,
I can see what is meant by Air Force Blue.

Now I really don't want to be a bore
But I'm much inclined to write a few more.
So many I like have been cast in the bin;
Examples, I wonder, of original sin?
The rest may be far from state of the art
And some dismissed as mere bleeding heart,
But sometimes I must let my feelings rip,
Even at the risk of shouldering a chip.

I like my verses to bring a smile
And I do poke fun just once in a while
But sardonic humour can havoc wreak
And tongues be hurtful held in cheek.
Acerbic wit is a cruel thing
And comic verse should hide no sting.
Nothing like that would I intend
For I would never seek to offend,
But I can't deny I've a wicked streak
And my resolution is all too weak ...
So, when you laugh and say "How true!",
Think a while .....for it could be you.

AEROBATICS

A lazy climb in a clear blue sky;
The fields so small up here so high.
Sunlight shining on silvery wings
Painted with those familiar rings.
Then down and down at increasing rate.
Throttle pushed hard right up to the gate.
The stick comes back and I feel the 'g'
Though I'm as gentle as I can be.
Even so, it all goes dark
As Newton's notions make their mark.
Over the top at a slower pace:
A perfect arc with effortless grace.
A downward swoop
Completes the loop.

Up again with throttle wide;
Sit right back; enjoy the ride.
I slow right down to the point of the stall,
Stretch one foot .... we begin to fall.
A hanging pivot on the starboard wing ...
A good stall turn is a delicate thing.

A steep descent, then up again.
I'm on my back and right as rain.
Now I'll do my party call
Just when I'm on the point of stall.
I stamp on rudder, jerk back the stick
And round we go in a crazy flick,
But I catch it neatly after one time round
And ease the nose towards the ground.
Stick smoothly back to complete the loop
And yet another upward swoop.

On my back but I'll not wait
For my shoulder straps take all my weight.
The stick well forward as I half-roll out.
This is what flying's all about.

A shallow dive, a roll or two.
This is what I loved to do
When I was young and fancy-free.
Now look what has become of me,
But, deep inside this clapped-out frame,
There's part of me that's just the same.

AFTERTHOUGHTS

Acerbic wit has been my style,
Though I've not written for quite a while;
So why not have a change of tack,
Find something that my verses lack.
I'll do a Keats and go all green,
Tread woodland paths, the rural scene,
Or should I dare the dread M6,
Seek inspiration in the sticks,
The fells I knew as a little boy,
Another model for my ploy,
And there, in the northlands of my birth,
See if my words have any worth.
Yet I would see satanic mills
And not just yellow daffodils.
It's changes that I seek to make,
Though I could never do a Blake.

I've sung rude songs in far-off climes,
As Rudyard did in olden times,
Though the only mark that he can make
Is now to bake his well-known cake.
Of wartime days I've had my fill,
Long-gone friends remembered still.
Siegfried knew a thing or two
And Wilfred wept as poets do,
But I could write a great deal more,
Though you would think it all a bore,
So fears and thrills and loves and lust
Are memories left to gather dust.
Though now I'm old, set in my ways,
I still recall exciting days
When life was lived to the very full
And death lurked close to make his cull.

Now there's a problem clear to me,
What sort of a poet do I aim to be?
Poking fun to make folks smile,
Little barbs slid in with guile,
Mocking someone's funny ways,
Bitter tales of childhood days.
Does it matter what folks say?
For me there is no other way.
Not for me the music of words,
Sylvan glades and twittering birds,

Virgin maids with silken hair.
Lovelorn youths in dark despair,
Ancient myth and long Greek names,
Fairies playing foolish games.
I'll just write as I think fit,
A waspish sting and a bawdy wit.
And, if I'm shown in a poorish light,
As people tell me well I might,
Then I'll plead simple honesty
And admit you're right...it's really me.

ARDINGTON

A village schoolmaster I used to be
In the heart of Berkshire's lush country.
After wartime's wild, exciting days,
I loved those gentle country ways.
A restful place where time stood still;
Of derring-do I'd had my fill.
Cottages tied to the local squire,
Converse all in broadest shire,
Chocolate box and outside loos,
An oddly feudal place to choose.
We had a barn dance now and then,
Buxom women and jolly men.

Cricket played on the village green,
A truly idyllic rural scene.
On Bonfire Night, we all turned out;
Hot potatoes and children's shout.
The village pub was called The Boar's Head,
Nothing to eat but cheese and bread
But I drank my fill of lukewarm beer
And at the dartboard had no peer.
Though none aspired to a motorcar,
Shanks' pony could take us surprisingly far.

A schoolroom warmed by an iron stove,
Long, leaded windows, curtains mauve.
Nibs and inkwells, copperplate,
All together now, nine times eight.
Tiers of desks all screwed to the floor,
History, geography, so much more,
A piano to lead us all in song,
To Sweet Polly Oliver, we warbled along.
Under the shade of the chestnut tree,
All at ease, they listened to me.
To widen their world I was so keen,
Yet their schooling was done by the age of fourteen.

On Sunday, the squire had his very own pew
And his workers sang to my organ's cue.
On Armistice Sunday, my nervous hand
Was accompanied by the Wantage silver band.
And we sported our medals and we walked tall,
For so many there had answered the call.

Now gentrification has taken it's course;
The bourgeoisie has arrived in force.
Sons of the soil are no longer around:
Ex-captains of industry now abound.
Captains, Colonels,commanders too,
Who like to tell them what to do.

Walkers give way to the motor car
And the innkeeper yearns for a Michelin star

But perhaps what I remember best
Is that teaching earned a lot of respect
And I was always proud to be
A member of that community.

AS TIME GOES BY

I remember the time when I leapt out of bed,
In time to brief the squadron I led.
Never been known to get there late,
Into my kit and airborne by eight.
Dining in style in the Officers' Mess;
Bedtime then was anyone's guess,
For, though we were so prettily dressed,
Wild games put folly to the test.

Parties galore on the married patch;
Serious drinkers, hard to match,
All of us having the time of our lives,
Dancing and flirting with other blokes' wives.
Limbo dancing was all the rage
And the MO's wife had been on the stage.
Tall and slender and a dusky brown ...
Oh how she loved to go to town!

Twice a week for the rugby-mad
And, as a fifteen, we weren't too bad.
Whenever the game was played away,
We never got back till late in the day.
Cricket has never appealed to me
But other sports were there for free
And always someone on for a game
For all our ages were about the same.

From time to time, a course to do ...
The bachelor life for a week or two.
A game of snooker, prop up the bar;
Play some bridge, phone home from afar;
Never go on the razzle or stay out late ...
That's my story at any rate.

AUTUMN DAYS

The air is filled with seagulls' cries,
A rippling wave is born, then dies,
Lapping the pebbles at the water's edge,
Breaking gently on the jetty's ledge.
Tall, slender masts sway on the swell;
A-top each one, a tinkling bell.
The sun smiles warm from a cloudless sky
And pretty girls are passing by.

I sit with friends outside The Ship,
A pint in hand and froth on lip,
And talk of dead men we once knew;
Recall those days of derring-do.

We've reached the age when time has stopped,
The harvest of hopes already cropped,
For the best of our lives is in the past
And the sand in the glass is trickling fast,
But, for today, we ask no more
Than to sit at ease on a Devon shore,
Accept the lot that Fate has sent
And take no heed of his intent

Just three old men on a wooden seat
Dozing in the summer's heat.

BIRTHDAY GIRL

How can you be eighty, you sexy old thing!
You still turn my head, make my senses ring.
And, seeing you twinkle on those tiny feet,
Well, that is what I call a real treat.
We met when you were twenty-five
And danced through the night in a hectic jive.
Far from home, in Cairo's heat,
We lost ourselves to the music's beat.
Though those wartime days are far away,
To me, they're still like yesterday
And the face I see when you look at me
Is ever the girl who used to be.
When we go out and agree to meet
Outside a shop on a busy street,
My heart gives a leap and I 'm so proud
When that elfin figure appears in the crowd

I can't deny that we sometimes fight
And many would say it can't be right
But the ups and downs are all a part
When head competes with fiery heart.
People say we're cheese and chalk
And there's more to that than idle talk,
For I'll admit, without reserve,
You're far, far better than I deserve.
I know that I have sometimes strayed
And your despair a price to be paid.
"No one's perfect!" is so easy to say
But doesn't wipe anyone's tears away.
I've been so lucky that I met you,
A rock in my life and a lover true.

A couple of old fogeys at breakfast today
But the years are as nothing on this your birthday.
I see you now as I saw you then
And I'll love you still till Time says: "When!"

BLUE STOCKING

A kindly soul, a real good sort;
A D.Litt. by St. Hilda taught.
Not averse to pungent smells
But never rhymed with tinkling bells.
A faith that's of the simpler kind,
Even for a sharper mind.
For more than forty years she's been
An icon on the village scene.

Layer on layer with coat atop,
A patron of the charity shop.
Collecting sticks to fire her grate,
Working hard till very late.
Reading the lesson on Sunday morn,
Her warden's pew by time well worn.
In the knave on Saturday,
Scrubbing the layers of grime away.
Always with her usual verve:
A vicar's daughter, born to serve.
Well past three score years and ten,
There surely are no better men.

Her boon companion, always near,
"Come to Mummy, there's a dear".
And when her Mummy comes to tea,
She sits and whines upon her knee.

A character in the nicest way......
What more is there that one can say.

BOOKS

The shelves stretch clear from wall to wall,
Poems and classics, I've got them all.
Hazlitt and Swift, Walt Whitman too,
Essays to see a dull night through.
Shelley and Milton, Byron and Keats
And umpteen other bygone treats.
Jimmy Joyce, a very odd man:
Understand him if you possibly can.
Aldous Huxley all in green,
Side by side in a set of fourteen.

Soldiers and sailors of great renown,
Stars of the stage and screen noted down.
Heroes of Twickers and White Hart Lane,
Athletic feats remembered again,
And, bought when I was a raw sixteen,
The detective novels of Ellery Queen.
The Collins Classics in red leather coats,
The pages all marked with my student notes;
Paper all yellowed and font so small,
And yes, it's true, I have read them all.
But cross my heart and hope to die
If I should ever tell a lie ...
It's many a year since I raised my arm
To reach the pages of Animal Farm.

The lurid tales of E.A.Poe,
My prize of seventy years ago.
Angel Pavement of '48,

A northern culture I can rate.
Warplanes of The Second World War ...
So full of memories still quite raw.
A Guide to The Teaching of Modern Maths ...
So many well remembered paths.
A wall of books no longer read ...
So ostentatious it's been said
But those pages teem with life for me,
Hide pictures only I can see.

BY THE SEASIDE

I know a place that likes to boast
The best fish and chips on the north-west coast,
And Kevin and Tracy would no doubt agree
That Blackpool's the place where they'd most like to be.
The tang of the sea and the hot dog stand,
The Empire Ballroom with its resident band.
Dodgems for people who cannot drive,
A place where they can really feel alive.

Candy floss and sticks of rock.
The Big Dipper's swooping, screaming shock.
Feeding the ducks in Stanley Park.
Sloppy kisses in the Ghost Train dark.
Dancing on the pier in the afternoon.
Young lovers blissfully over the moon.
The noise and glitter of the Golden Mile.
A promenade bench to rest a while.
Your fortune told by Gypsy Rose;
A swarthy skin and a ring in her nose.

Mums and dads and their noisy brood.
Thermos flasks and shrink-wrapped food.
A canvas windbreak to mark their space.
Sun beating down on bright red face.

Comic postcards with a fat lady's bum ...
Really, a bit like our Tracy's mum.
From the top of the Tower, there's a splendid view:
The sea or the gasworks; it's up to you.
Down below, it's dancing once more,
Where white-suited Reggie once rose through the floor.

In the cheap B and B, the breakfast won't wait
And you won't get in if you come back too late,
Though how can you keep any note of the time
When you're into your umpteenth lager and lime?
Still, there's always the beach with its lovely soft sand;
The beating of any naff tropical strand
So Kevin and Tracy can snuggle up tight
And enjoy the rest of their loving last night.

But, when Autumn brings its darkening nights,
There'll be a coach trip from Salford to visit THE LIGHTS

.CHATTERBOX

Hullo, Polly, I'm phoning to say
I can't make the WI thing today.
I was so looking forward to Harriet's tale
Of the doings at the annual Red Cross sale.
The strangest thing I ever heard
Was her sighting of the circling Woozo bird.
How could it do that, I want to know ...
And what a peculiar place to go!
Her graphic account of fertility rites
Has kept me awake for umpteen nights.
John, you know, has always been shy
But I'd be perfectly willing to give it a try.
I thought of writing away for some gear
But I don't want to frighten the poor little dear.

Talking of which, the new vicar's unwed.

Oh dear, a rhyme has got stuck in my head.
But, there I go, ever thinking the worst.
But, remember, my dear, 'twas I saw him first.
He's ever so young and very sweet.
He's quite swept the wrinklies off their feet.
So, how about it, Polly my girl?
Pop round next week and we'll give him a whirl.

I've made some chutney for the village fete.
I'll set up my stall by the west paddock gate.
John laughed like a drain and gave me a tickle
'Cos the silly old thing likes to call me "Pickle".
Between me and thee, so keep it dark,
That's all too often been close to the mark.

Toby was expelled from Radley last week
For being rather rude to a snotty-nosed beak.
"Never mind, my sweet;" I said to him,
"I don't think you're really dim.
I danced with a chap at the last Hunt Ball
Who promised you a place at Teddy Hall.
I said, of course, that you'd love to go
And I quite enjoyed the quid pro quo."

By the way, my dear, I've been meaning to ring:
On Friday week, are you doing anything?
Come round for dinner; your Crispin too.
Half eight for nine... does that suit you?
We're having the new people from the Manor House.
I've heard that the wife is a bit of a mouse,
But she's still an Hon, so she's one of us,
So do your best to make a fuss.

Didn't see you at the Tompkins' lunchtime do,
Though I doubt it would really have suited you.
You know what a wine snob you tend to be
And the plonk that they served was just like gnats' pee.

What d'you expect?" I heard John say,
In his own inimitable, witty way.
Mind you, mine host had a certain rough charm
And a discreet little dabble would do me no harm.

There's the doorbell ...got to go!
I think it's the postman; the tall one you know.
I asked him to ring if he'd like a cup
But he'll need a long spoon if he decides to sup ...

CHILDHOOD

I'm Northern bred, a trueborn Scouse.
Born and raised in a humble house.
When I was rising seven or eight,
I ran to school with carefree gait.
On pavements bare, a mile each way,
I did it four times every day.
The Carnegie Library was Aladdin's cave
And hours of pleasure it freely gave.

The maps were coloured in Empire red,
Battles were fought by knights long dead.
Page after page of fairy tale,
Of myth and legend, the life of the whale.
Animals of the wild, birds of the air.
So much to read....but no one to share,
And now and then a library seat
At a lantern lecture for a treat.
The ships in the river were all nearby;
Their foghorns at night were my lullaby.
Melancholy boom on the cold night air
As, like great beasts, they slid from their lair.

I often went down to the Pier Head,
A bottle of water and a slice of bread.
Elder Dempster, Blue Funnel, Holt and Cunard;

To name White Star was not very hard.
Blue Peter raised, I knew they'd sail
As I gazed, round-eyed, 'gainst the landing-stage rail.
Though poor we were and not well-fed,
A world of wonder yet filled my head.

The Premier cinema at the end of our street ...
For tuppence a ticket, we queued for a seat.
Snaking slowly, slowly round the side,
A beaten, despairing human tide.
My weary father, my hand held tight ...
Could he be here, I'd see him right!
My mother too, her head held proud,
Trying to keep us above the crowd.

Maudlin you may think this to be
But starkly real it was to me
And I cannot help but now recall
Those to whom I owe my all.

CLASSIC F.M.

"Welcome all to your favourite show
Of classical music, soft and low.
I'll woo you with my seductive voice
And play the discs of your very own choice.
We'll start with Nabucco, that thing about slaves,
For Brenda of Braintree's rapturous raves.
Kevin of Camden has asked my advice ...
He's heard a piece that he thinks is quite nice.
It's a funny French name, if you know what I mean:
By a group called Four A with a lead called Rasseen.
Darren of Droylsden likes movements slow;
Mantovani playing Mahler, he wants to know.
Tracy of Tooting's a safer bet:
Have we heard of piece called the Trout Quintet?

Barry of Balham's a Beethoven buff ...
That bit with the storm will do well enough.
Karen of Colchester is learning to play
So her mum wants a bit of the Moonlight today.
Now here's a listener who's close to our hearts ...
Colonel Bagshot's never been one for the arts,
But he heard a good tune the other day
And that's the one he'd like us to play.
He's been told it's by Elgar but he's not too sure
But, for England at Twickers, it proved a good cure.
Elsie from Eltham loves package tours:
Wants "something Italian, but the choice is all yours. "
Puccini's the name that springs to my mind ...
Che Gelida Manina's the one for your kind.

I'll have a break, take time to reflect ...
I wonder what I'll have to croon about next.
I'll opt for Bach, the Double Violin
But Air on the G-String can push its way in.
And, for those who tell us of rainbows they've chased,
There's a bit of Chopin we've easily traced.
Mars is the choice of Holst that I play
And Elgar means Nimrod or that thing by du Pré.
Sharon from Sale's getting on a bit
But once saw a film that became a great hit
When Trevor and Celia were lovers shy:
Rachmaninov will help her to have a good cry.
Now, what on earth am I thinking about.
I've forgotten Tchaikovsky, a sure-fire sell-out.
For those heart-rending strings in the Pathetique,
Glenn Miller's the man that some listeners seek,
For his was the Story of a Starry Night
Under Hammersmith Palais' twinkling strobe light,
Though that was the pop of an earlier day
And not for what my masters pay.

I was chosen, my voice a soft caress,
To play music that eases a listener's stress
And to show to people what music can mean
When perhaps it's not part of their usual scene.
If they want an analysis of sonata form,
There are other programmes where that's the norm.
Though the same bits are played again and again,
I do hope my listeners will get a yen
For rather more than I can play ...
So have no need of me one day.

COMBAT

The adrenaline's pumping and I'm wet with pee
For I know that the choice is him or me.
The aircraft's juddering on the point of the stall.
And it's going to be a very close call,
But I've got inside him and I press the tit,
And now he's really in the shit.
My cockpit's full of cordite fumes
And the airframe shakes with the cannons' booms,
But I haven't got the deflection right
And he pulls away right out of sight.
Where's he gone? I straighten out
And my navigator gives an anguished shout,
For the port wing's now a mass of flame.
And surely I'm the one to blame;
So it's rudder and aileron into the turn
While the wing out there continues to burn.
Tracer streams past on the starboard side
And there's nowhere at all that I can hide.
It's round and round in a deadly game,
But now it's not at all the same,
For he's the hunter and I'm the prey
And he's the winner on the day.

A still blue sea just feet below,
Quietly waiting for the wing to blow.
I cannot think, my mind's gone numb;
I know for sure my time has come.
The instruments are spinning with excessive g,
The stick's in my stomach, far back as can be.
If I pull any harder, we'll surely stall
And I know I'm riding for a fall.
I'm in despair, can't shake him off
And now one engine starts to cough.
I've got to ditch but will he be kind?
I have no choice; I make up my mind....
Jettison the hatch, pull the throttles close.
As the speed drops off, I raise the nose.
We skim the surface, bounce once or twice,
Then the fight is over, all in a trice.
The water pours in as I scramble out.
See three 88's still circling about.
F for Freddie, all fiery glow,
Lifts his tail and slides below.
We're left alone to our sorry plight
And the imagined terrors of the night.

COMPANION

On balmy days, we go for walks,
Though I'm the only one who talks,
For I'm inclined to think aloud
And never one to seek a crowd.
The two of us a happy pair,
Ambling along without a care.

Fields and footpaths we like best.
Against stone walls we pause to rest.
She leans on me, I stroke her hair

So she can tell I really care.
I know that she will never stray,
Faithful still since many a day.

We might pop in to the local inn;
I'll have a nog or two of gin,
Sit by the fire on a wooden pew....
Such pleasures now so very few.
Samantha snores by a sizzling log,
And asks no more.....for she's only a dog.

COUNTING SHEEP

It's often said that counting sheep
Is just the way to get to sleep
But, when I get past ninety-two,
My mind seeks other things to do
And, all too often, brings recall
To things I've done that now appal.

If I believed in Heaven's gate,
I'd dread to contemplate my fate
But, at the time, I didn't care
And now it's all beyond repair,
But, as I lie in bed at night,
These memories strive to reach the light,
To burst the bubble of self-esteem
And deny all hope of guileless dream,

My eyelids close to another time;
It's all so real ... I'm in my prime
And, once again, I have a ball...
I haven't really changed at all.
For in my dream, I'm still the same:
I wake once more to yet more blame.

COUNTRY LIFE

I used to live on a city street.
Pavements thudding with frantic feet.
I'd open the door and step outside
To rain-slicked flagstones, smooth and wide.
Where people hurried to and fro,
All alert and set to go,
And little groups of laughing girls,
All mini-skirt and tossing curls,
Cast a knowing look at us,
Waiting for the next red bus,
And housewives made their questing stops
At lots and lots of little shops.
There were few who knew my name
Yet there was company all the same,
For I could feel that I was part
Of that great city's beating heart,
Where no one tried to coax from me
Those private things they need not see.

Now I'm part of the rural scene,
Where roofs are thatched and grass is green,
And my garden's like a chocolate box,
With a climbing rose and hollyhocks.
Of a living soul there's not a sign
For village life is in decline.
A dying pub, no bus, no shop.
It seems that life has come to a stop.
If I go for a stroll, it's the same old thing:
A muddy lane and rooks on the wing,
Empty fields, a mournful cow,
Some distant sheep, a grunting sow.
Lady Muck on a big grey mare,
Half-raised hand and a haughty stare.

To show how dotty I can be,

I've even begun to talk to me.
And me tells me to get a grip
And not to let my spirits dip........
Oh, there's a weed, I'll get my hoe;
Then sit and watch my oak tree grow.

CREDO

The candles are lit and there's a funny smell;
I hear the sound of a tinkling bell.
The parson drops a bobbing knee:
All rather studied it seems to me.
Clad in red and gold brocade:
Gestures all a tool of his trade.
But he is neither humble nor poor
And comes across as a pedantic boor.
He parrots the words he knows so well:
How the good go to Heaven and the bad to Hell;
How those who a path to righteousness seek
Should give to the poor and help the weak,
But I would believe a great deal more
If he could seem what he stood for;
Minding how it all began
And not such a peacock of a man.

He parades his learning for us to hear;
Greek and Hebrew are all made clear.
The historical context is painted in;
A passing mention made of sin.
Exhortations with arms outflung,
Then tedious psalms are pointedly sung.
Words without meaning are bandied about.
How am I to work them out?
God Incarnate, Father, Son,
Holy Ghost, the Three-in-One,
Great Jehovah, Trinity.

Empty words for the likes of me.
The dead will rise: what can that mean?
Will I return as a boy of eighteen?
It's only an allegory but what's to believe?
What devious spells does religion weave!

I'd like to believe but my brain rebels
And rejects the myths that religion sells.
I'm all for a creed that's based on love;
Not a cross for a symbol but a pure white dove.
Humility and charity I do admire,
Though to suchlike heights I can't aspire.
My church would turn from life's mad rush:
Have nought to do with shove and push:
A catalyst for a better life,
A world more free of hate and strife ...
Not looking back to a distant past,
Or seeking salvation in a Lenten fast.

I can't abide the bread and wine,
People queuing in a doleful line;
Eyes downcast in pious mien,
Smiling faces never seen.
"This is my blood which is shed for you"
How dare I sip if that be true?

Let us show that there's still hope,
Try not to cringe, to sniff and mope;
Raise our voice in joyous song,
Resolve to do no witting wrong
And, just maybe, our common will
May seal a gap the Church can't fill.

And, when I die, the line is drawn;
There'll never be a second dawn,
Though there may be some part of me
That lives in someone's memory.

DIY

I'm apt to get crazes I can't leave alone;
Can't stop at all once the seed has been sown.
I'm not fond of gardening but I like building walls ...
Am still mixing mortar as eventide falls.
I'll lay a few flags round the kitchen door
And, day after day, I'll lay a few more.
Then my loved one cries, with senses bereft,
"Oh no, just look, there's no garden left!"
I come into the house and put up the odd shelf
And, whilst I'm really enjoying myself,
I'll panel a few walls with some tongue and groove,
Though it won't be an asset when we have to move.
Then my true love denies me a share of her bed
For she says that our home has turned into a shed.
I tear it all down ... hauled over the coals
For leaving a web of neat little holes.
So, it's out with the filler and I'm happy again;
Pottering about, feeling right as the rain,
But, all the time, the woman I love
Is fussing around with an angry shove,
Wielding a mop where I want to go
And interrupting my work with an anguished "No, no!"

Now the wall's to be painted a suitable hue
And I've chosen a greenish-grey sort of blue.
To be on the safe side, I tell my love true ....
But with those tins of paint, I am told what to do.
So I paint the wall in a brilliant white.....
When you're certain to lose, it's best not to fight,
But I forget to put a sheet on the floor
And the wall-to-wall carpet's not brown any more,
But I have a bright thought to smooth tears away......
I'll lay a new floor in maple parquet.
Tactfully, I try my idea for size......
What she rudely suggests would bring tears to my eyes.

I've tried to explain to my long-suffering wife
That a man needs a hobby to enjoy retired life
But I'm beginning to think that a man obsessed
May well be regarded as a bit of a pest,
So I've decided to do what many think worse
And make a real effort to write comic verse.

DAD

He came to us a few years late,
A little surprise from a fickle Fate.
Two's just fine, we'd both agreed;
That's all that we would ever need,
But, four years on, and out he popped.
Oh, what a clanger I had dropped!

A moody soul he proved to be,
And he didn't look at all like me.
Though bright as a button, he hated school
And did his best to play the fool.
Stayed out late...where did he go?
We would be the last to know.
His funny friends filled us with dread.
Did he lead or was he led?
How could we bring this to a halt?
It surely wasn't all our fault!
The magistrate wipes his gold pince-nez
And decides how much we have to pay,
For that, you see, is your sorry lot
When your kids are avidly going to pot.

But then he met this wild young thing,
With whom he had a wild young fling.
Now they've achieved what many miss:
Thirty years of carefree bliss.
The Andes, the Alps, the hills of Nepal;

Amazon, Congo; they know them all.
Birds of a feather, peas in a pod;
What many paths those two have trod!
They've followed their luck wherever it's led;
It's all about heart and to hell with the head!
Tequila in Mexico, nuts in Brazil
And often, no doubt, the happiness pill.
A meal in the jungle where no white man goes;
Their host a savage, a bone through his nose.
White water rafting, so devil-may-care!
Bareback riding at a Romany fair,
Scuba diving in tropical seas,
Para-gliding in the high Pyrenees.

Middle-aged hippies, lovers still,
Now comes the time to pay the bill
Yesterday another day:
Today a dreadful toll to pay.
The telephone shrills....just three words said:
A choking sob, then "Liz is dead!"
I'm lost for words: I feel so bad,
For after all, I am his Dad.
So long away, he needs me now,
But, sad to say, I don't know how!

DEAD-RECKONING

We're lolling about on Sardinian sand ,
A can of beer in everyone's hand.
It's late at night but the weather's warm
And living in tents has become the norm.
Then, all of a sudden, there's a bit of a stay;
The Intelligence Officer has something to say.
"All pilots who've flown this month at night
Report with their navs to the ops room site."
An armoured column is moving on Rome
And we, with our rockets, are to send them off home.
We're to fly on our own at fifty feet ...
List to the whisper of our engines' soft beat.

It's dark as pitch and I whisper my prayers;
The runway's lit by a few feeble flares.
When we're safely away and well out to sea.
My navigator gives the first heading to me.
I can't see a thing in the inky dark.
Flying so low is far from a lark

Over there on the right, a fireworks display.
"That's Elba, our turn," I hear Alan say.
He gives me a course and we gain some height
Soon Italy's coast is lost in the night.
I sense a certain growing unease
And a dampness snakes slowly down to my knees.
From the back there comes not the slightest peep;
I'm beginning to think he's gone off to sleep.
And then, I see Elba again on the right;
The gunners don't hit us, though try as they might.
Then Alan comes up with a change or two.
Here's Elba again ... it cannot be true!
But I've got to put my trust in him
For I can't fly just on my very own whim.

Silence from the back is annoying me
For I've no idea where we can be
And, when Elba comes up ... on the left this time ...
I realise that Alan is far from his prime.
I should never have let him make a start
For, without any doubt, he's pissed as a fart.

The radio suddenly bursts into life,
Just as I'm beginning to fear for my life.
O joy of joy, what news to arrive,
We're going to get out of this mess alive!
The weather's clamping and we must abort.
Another battle...though hardly well fought .
It's already too bad to return to base
But an airstrip in Corsica might just suit our case.
So we fire our rockets at a blameless sea ...
It seems such a dreadful waste to me,
And, after another problem or two,
We land at Borgo, a very relieved crew.
And, while poor Alan's throwing up in the back,
I heave myself out with my parachute pack.

I can't really blame him for leaving his mark
For I'm doing the same thing nearby in the dark.

DESERT ISLAND DISCS

I'm on my tod in paradise.
No chattering tongues, no staring eyes.
Just silver sand and calm blue sea.
No one here but little me.
Yet I'm not really all alone:
I've got my wind-up gramophone.

I remember my favourite jazz club scene
Where bright young things would primp and preen.
Ben Webster brings it back to me;
'Where Are You?' provides the key.

A piano gallops in my mind;
A silken tenor close behind.
Fischer-Dieskau sings for me,
Sweetly, sweetly, tenderly.
'Im Fruhling' is the song I need.......
Schubert's tune is bliss indeed.

I've worn a shirt striped white and green
And to the valleys I have been
And played against Treorchy men.
Please sing 'Myfanwy' once again.

Who can write like Ludwig van?
Trios for the thinking man.
Head and shoulders o'er the rest.
'The Archduke' is the very best.

Ella for me can do no wrong,
Though, yes, she tarried just too long,
So remind me of that Small Hotel
That I recall she sang so well.

When it comes to Dvorak, I'm in a fix.
Is the Piano Quintet my Number Six?
No, into the quartets I'd sooner delve:
Op 96, the Number 12.

Chopin has his delicate way;
Easy listening, hard to play.
Op 27, the Number 2,
Nocturne to see a bad night through.

Elgar generally means du Prè
Or the Albert Hall on closing day,
But I'll just bid for a gentler piece:
'Ave Verum' if you please.

Oh dear, I haven't got another vote,
Yet there are still more names to note.
Faure's Requiem wrings a tear;
A trifle hackneyed now, I fear.
Mendelssohn always appeals to me:
The Piano Trio in the key of D.

Shostakovitch pounds his Russian beat
But the Piano Concerto is a treat.
Schumann, Schubert, Grieg and Brahms,
Tchaikovsky for a lilt that charms.
 Rachmaninov if I want to cry,
Though Mahler's not a bad stand-by.
Bach's left out as rather staid
For a tropic isle with little shade.

Dido takes her time to die ...
Purcell too can make me cry.
Let's break the mould and make it nine
And, so that I don't fret and whine,
Let's up to a much more pulsing beat

And pander to my dancing feet.
Count Basie is the man I'll choose
To play for me 'The How Long Blues'.

Now, for that other thing to take,
A small request I'd like to make.
Music's charms I have in spades
But, ere too long, the interest fades.
Adam's lonely on this Eden shore.
There's something that he needs much more.
I know there will be no reprieve
But, I beg of you, please give me Eve.

DOT.COM

Log on, log off, click left, click right.
I've lost the work I did last night.
Document, folder, file and font.
What more could any student want?
Whilst fiddling about with the first line's height,
The whole darn page has moved to the right,
And another problem I have to face:
The text has all gone double space,
And it's really quite beyond my ken
Why the font has shrunk from twelve to ten.

I call the tutor ... a very nice man.
He'll sort it out if anyone can.
Click, click, click and click, click, click.
Oh my, he's such a clever dick!
But what he's done I'll never know
For I didn't dare to stem his flow.

I try the e-mail but it's just the same;
The server doesn't even know my name.
Google, Yahoo, Hotmail, Jeeves;

A new name comes as the last one leaves,
But, if William Gates is the name from Hell,
It can't compare with the devil named Dell!

DREAMS

Of what do you dream in the dark of night,
Tucked up in bed, so warm and tight?
Long-lost youth becomes so real,
What wild emotions you can feel!
Pangs of first-love, a gentle kiss,
Country walks that promise bliss,
The roar of the crowd on a Twickers day
As you beguile them with your play.
The glittering gong pinned on your chest,
For you're the bravest and the best.
Flights of fancy far from real
But my, how good they make you feel!

Or are you full of self-reproach;
Sins much better not to broach.
Harsh words that blighted many a life,
A vicious bent to foster strife.
Accepting love: none given back;
Deriding virtues that you lack.

Or are your dreams a time of fear,
When unknown terrors seem so near?
You wake at last all wet with fright
But there's no comfort in the night,
For there's a shadow on the wall,
Ever closer ... so, so tall.

Sit up in bed; switch on the light
And pray you dream no more tonight.

EGO

I've always wanted to be the best,
Make gods perform at my behest.
I did my homework as a lad,
Avoided things my mum thought bad,
Gave my all on the rugby pitch,
Though I was small..... oh life's a bitch!
Learned to foxtrot like a pro,
Met daring girls, put on a show,
Went to war at raw eighteen,
A knife-edged crease and buttons clean;
Yet not prepared to toe the line
For intellects less sharp than mine,
Gave my all in every way,
Let raging passion have its way,
Fell in love so many times,
Cast my seed in far-off climes

Earned my wings and cut a dash,
Ever the first to have a bash,
Couldn't wait to fly on ops,
Thought the war was quite the tops.
Used my commission to impress
When elevated from the Sergeants' Mess.
So sure of what was due to me,
How did I miss that DFC?
Still couldn't do what I was told,
Wanted to be the pilot bold,
So I was often in disgrace
Because I never knew my place,

But I climbed the ladder all the same
And a Whitehall Warrior I became.
I flew my desk with great panache:
With tight-rolled brolly, cut a dash.

Clad again in a suit of blue,
Told other chaps what they must do
But still could not accept the norm:
Always hated to conform.
So, in the end, I opted out,
Let my career go up the spout.
So now I'm free to do my thing
And let my fancy take its wing.
Yet I still miss the days of yore
And have become a frightful bore,
Telling how it used to be,
How it was for me, me, me!

EVENSONG

The sopranos shrill, the basses boom,
The altos should be in another room.
The organ sounds but not quite right;
The organist cannot read by sight.
Why is Marge in such a rage?
Could Fred have missed another page?
Is there a solo descant there ?
How avant-garde: an atonal air.
Psalm 42 is for today.
We'll drone it in our dreary way.
Of Mag and Nunc we are more sure.
We follow the pointing clear and pure.
Ron announces "Three four eight".
"No, no!" cries Helen,"Wait, wait, wait!"
"I've changed my mind though you don't know"
"We'll have instead the Three four oh".

Ronald knits his noble brow
And murmurs words as he knows how,
The singing dies at an alarming rate:
Fred's still playing three four eight.

On and on and on he goes,
Fourteen verses at the close.

Now Ron's well into his stride,
The arms outflung, the jokes well tried.
The ladies laugh, they'd like to scream
"O darling man, you're such a dream."
Now the last hymn's time has come;
Ron, in doubt, remains quite schtum.
Helen takes the chancel floor.
Loud she cries, "It's One three four".
Ronald smiles his secret smile,
Five ladies faint right in the aisle.
He's reminded of a Rugby ditty
But won't repeat it ...what a pity!
For tales of Nell and naughty Pete
Would bring those ladies to their feet.

Good old Ron has done his bit;
We've heard the last of Celtic wit.
Now Fred is poised to do his thing;
He's going to make the ivories sing.
Sweet music's drowned in clamourous chat
But Fred, all peeved wants none of that.
Never one to sulk and pout,
He pulls his loudest stops full out
And, though they've put him to the test,
It's organist Fred who comes off best.

EXTRA-MURAL STUDIES

Why should our feelings cause a stir,
Just because we're Miss and Sir?
All the same, we'll be discreet
When warily choosing the times to meet.
Though, should I touch her trailing hand,
I'd feel that alien golden band.

At three, the tumult dies away,
To mark the close of our working day,
A dedicated teacher I'm known to be,
So it's not the end for such as me.
With little smiles, the staff all leave......
Is my heart so clearly on my sleeve?

Now if you thought I'd be alone,
That's not the path that I have shown.
Ah, the exquisite pain of Cupid's rack!
But it's only a rick in the small of my back,
For there's never a gain without the pain
As my studies strive for a higher plane.

I'm back at home at half past six
And once again I'm up to my tricks.
Who will choose to comfort me,
This star-crossed lover plain to see
Is it lovely Chardonnay
Who seeks to lure me far astray
Or red-blooded Merlot with pouting lips
Who offers more than precious sips?
Or Chianti, the girl with the sensuous mouth......
Black-haired siren from the sunny south.

Who drinks water when nectar's free?
Certainly, never a toper like me.
But, when the Blue Nun comes strutting her stuff,
I'll settle tonight for a bit of rough.

FAITH

When I was a boy and still very small,
I went with my mam to a place called Sun Hall.
Could you find such a name, if you were to try,
For a dismal building where trams rattled by?
Yet not so strange for ordinary folk
Who knew too well the weight of life's yoke.
What matter what the preacher said
Or any of the lessons that he read,
But that joyous singing I do recall;
For Sankey and Moody they gave their all.

I've been in churches with smoky smells
And listened to tinkling of off-stage bells,
Where the vicar's dressed up in silk and gold wire
And the only singing's from a well-trained choir.
I've listened to parsons in all shapes and guise:
From the charismatic to the insufferably wise.
I've been bored to death by the original Greek
When it's a path to true faith that I really seek.
The Hebrew context has been explained to me
When it's a different light that I want to see.
So many who want me to do what's right ...
Get out in the world and fight the good fight.
Can't any single one of them see
They're not getting through at all to me.
They have a problem, I'll freely admit,
For you can't acquire faith by wisdom or wit.
So they're really on to a losing streak
As they prepare their sermons as week follows week.
For faith and reason are poles apart:
It's not for the mind but only the heart.
So, when I think of that long-gone Sun Hall:
Sun of my Soul ... perhaps that says it all.

FIGHTER PILOT

Wings on my breast and stripes on my sleeve,
Girls to love and girls to leave.
Pints to drink and songs to sing,
Live for today; oh that's the thing!

A deckchair out in the summer sun,
The klaxon sounds and we're at the run.
The undercart's up with a heavy thud,
The huntsman's got the scent of blood.

For this is such a jolly game
And one in which I'll make my name.
An eager boy in a world of men,
Excited, I climb through angels ten.

My senses tingle, I feel the thrill.
I'm spoiling for a fight and I want a kill ...
A fearful noise, the flames all red
And now I'm one of Our Glorious Dead.

GOURMET

In my early years, my appetite grew;
Tripe and trotters and Irish stew.
Black puddings and brawn you may find strange
But our bread was made on the coal-fired range.
The goose was plucked in a bath on the floor
And goose grease kept for throats that got sore,
And, just to keep my workings right,
It was brimstone and treacle every Saturday night.
I've oft since wondered from what time past
Was such a devilish title cast.

At raw eighteen, I went to war;

Was always the first to ask for more.
Bangers and mash was my kind of stuff,
And oh the heaven of stodgy plum duff!
A naval man who knew me quite well
Thought of a bird on the ocean swell.
No compliment that, or so I've heard,
For the gannet's a notoriously greedy bird.
I've grown more careful about what I eat,
Though I do have a penchant for all red meat.
I can't stand the sight of creme brulee
And sticky puds were for yesterday.
Steak and kidney is a favourite dish
But just one bone and I'm finished with fish.
What really brings my blood to the boil
Is food all drizzled in that olive oil,
So dishes prepared by celebrity chefs
Too often resemble a grease-laden mess.

I'm fond of cheese and a cracker or two.
Caerphilly or Cheshire or Cheddar will do.
I know a man who likes Roquefort
But only, I'm sure, because it costs more.
Cheap plonk is always my choice of wine;
No sniffing or swirling if the taste is fine.
I don't hold a glass by its thin little stem,
Regard those who do as another of them.
To be a gourmet I'd never claim
But everyone's taste is not the same
And who's to say whose taste is best:
Why yours is better than the rest?
Gourmand or gourmet, it's for me to say
What I choose to eat and drink each day.

HOLIDAYS

It's July and hot on our city street,
But term is over and I'm in for a treat
For we're off to a land of lakes and fell
That Mam, as a girl, had known so well.
Our needs are small so we travel light;
Just one battered case will see us right.
A rattling tram takes us both downtown
To Lime Street station, all grimy and brown,
Where hissing monsters are a boy's delight,
But not too close or I might take fright.
We pull away in a cloud of steam
And tippety-tat to a rural dream.
Fields and farms and sheep and cows
And pairs of horses pulling ploughs.

Lancaster's where we catch the bus.
It's market day.......such an exciting fuss.
We stop at each village along the way
And women with baskets enjoy the day.
There's gossip and banter, a friendly air.
My mother's broad brogue is one they all share.
At Kirkby Lonsdale, the bus turns about;
By the market cross, we all get out.
Then my mother and I, with weary gait,
Climb the winding hill of old Michelgate.
Halfway up is where we shall stop,
Where Auntie Sarah keeps a village shop.
There's a stone-flagged floor and bottles of sweets,
Bacon and hams and all sorts of treats.
When darkness falls, round an oil lamp we sit
And my climb to my bed is by candlelight lit.

I'm free to come and go as I please.
I swim in the Lune though it's fit to freeze,
Skim smooth flat pebbles to the other side.

Beyond Devil's Bridge, it's deep but not wide.
Then up to the farm to help with the hay .
Perhaps I can lead the old horse today.
And, now and again, very late at night,
It's fishing for trout in the pale moonlight.
Mam talks to people she knew at school,
For to chat in the street seems the general rule
And, though there's so little that we can afford,
I'm left on my own but I'm never bored.

I drove up there some months ago
But found a place I didn't know.
The Lune's crystal waters had turned a dark brown,
Cars nose-to-tail polluted the town,
The Westmorland brogue had turned to Scouse
And our village shop was now a house.
I stood and stared at that house on the hill
And, just for a moment, time seemed to stand still
And I was just a little boy
An innocent still and full of joy.
The clouds of war long years ahead,
No doubts or worrying in my head.

Then, all too soon, the moment passed,
For retrospect lies to the last
And halcyon years we used to know
Are painted in a rosy glow.
Despair and passion often run wild
Though seldom seen through the eyes of a child,
And the rural idyll that I strove to see
May well have been true ... but only for me.

HOUSE-TRAINED

I am a slob, I must admit;
There's not another word for it.
I drop my crumbs and spill my tea.
Where I sit is plain to see,
And over there, behind the door,
I've thrown a bit of apple core.
I get up late, don't make the bed,
Stretch my arms and scratch my head.
Don't change my shirt or match my socks
Or comb my wild and flowing locks.
I make a point of keeping clean,
Though you can tell where I have been
For round the bath there is a mark,
Long and rough and rather dark.

It's autumn now and leaves still fall:
Are lying thick around the hall,
For, though I try to wipe my feet,
My efforts never seem complete.
The leaves are scattered, crisp and small,
But I don't really mind at all,
For, if I clear them all away,
They'll still come back another day.

As for food, I just get by........
I'm happy with a shop-bought pie.
Burgers, beans, spaghetti rings,
Pizzas, chips and take-away things
Cans of beer to wash it down,
Special brew or a modest brown.
Straight from the can is how I sup.......
I try to avoid the washing-up.
It's been like this for a week or two.
What on Earth am I to do,
For the wife's due back from her trip away

And there'll be merry Hell to pay!
Though tomorrow will be as I like it to be,
When there's someone here to look after me.

HOUSE FOR SALE

I've done some painting and the furniture's new,
Knocked down a wall to see straight through.
On the kitchen extension, we should have spent more
And my feet get cold on the quarry-tiled floor.
The spiral stairs look as glam as I'd thought
But the king-size bed we should never have bought.
The picture windows are a sight to see
But the planners have asked for a word with me.
It doesn't matter for I've itchy feet;
Am thinking of moving to another street,
So I'm off to the agents to do a good deal,
Looking far less eager than I really feel.

Here's a place of up-market repute,
Manned by a gent in an expensive tweed suit.
"It's three percent" ... I edge to the door ...
"Then Country Life will be quite a lot more."
The next one's part of a national group
And the baggy blue suit is stained with soup.
The lurid tie is an awesome sight
But the socks are gleaming in brilliant white.
I give him a smile for he's obviously keen
Though he doesn't look more than a gauche eighteen.
"From three percent ... that's cheap for today"
Does he really think I was born yesterday?
I look and smile, then turn away ...
"But there's room for discussion," he hastens to say.
We chat for a while, then go on our way,
Agree one and a half and no more to pay.

So we clean up the house, make it all spick and span,
Slap on the white paint, use can after can.
The pooch is dispatched to the garden shed.
The front of the Aga's no longer his bed.
If the wet patch upstairs seems a bit untoward,
I'll do my thing with some plasterboard.
The wife's roasting coffee, the real stuff you know,
And the fire in the lounge has at last got a glow.
We've picked our time with a great deal of thought,
For next door is on tour with the drum kit he's bought.

The stage is set for our curtain call:
"Come in Mrs Jones, step into the hall ..."

HOUSE-HUNTING

They say that moving's a time of stress
And people can get into a terrible mess
But I've always found it far from a bore
And I've done it a great many times before.
Oft it has been at The Queen's dictate
And I've had no choice for she wouldn't wait.
But, of the rest, I'm bound to say,
I've always looked forward to moving day.

First, decide where you want to live;
Then put the owners through the sieve,
Never believe a word they say;
Decide how much you want to pay.
Be nice to people whose houses you hate;
Beware of the dog as you walk through the gate.
Tread carefully through tangles of nettles and docks,
Try not to sneer at the agent's white socks.

Turn up at the time you're due to be met,
When the coffee's been ground and the log fire set.
Always remember to be very discreet
With the house-proud owners you're likely to meet,
And don't reveal what you intend to do
About tasteless things not appealing to you;
Jet-black ceilings may be all the rage
For other people of a certain age
And when the pooch throws up on your foot,
Try not to kick its fat little gut.

There's often a room you must take for read,
For the teenage son will still be in bed.
Be sure to enquire of his friend next door.
Guitarist or drummer ... then dally no more!
Make for the pub not far down the street,
Pop in for a pint where the locals meet.
It's often surprising what you will hear
When people are supping a convivial beer.
The important question is a delicate task:
"Why are you moving?" is the one to ask.
All too often is the answer a lie
But you can get to the truth if you really try.

If you find that they've recently run out of cash,
You know that you're clear to have a bash,
And they will give in without a fight,
Leaving a margin to put things right.

You can tear off the paper, put in a new sink,
Paint over the colours that make your eyes blink,
But remember well that important law ...
You can't do a thing about the people next door.

HOW ARE YOU?

It's been one of those days I know so well.
I've strained my back and it hurts like hell.
My blood pressure's up and I've taken my pill.
If a stroke doesn't get me, the side effects will.
I fart like a trooper but I can't perform,
Though twice a day was once my norm.
Don't get me wrong; I don't mean that ...
My orgasmic peaks have gone quite flat.
Someone's using a pneumatic drill ...
Or could it be my latest pill?
I tell the doc and he begins to smile,
For the crafty git is full of guile
And enjoys every bit of his jolly game
By writing me up for more of the same.
"How's your love life?" he dares to ask.
To remember at all is no mean task.
"Could the practice nurse improve my lot?" ...
Sadly, His Nibs thinks probably not.

Did I mention my eyes? I'm going blind.
Deaf as a post; it's such a bind.
I'm overweight by at least two stone,
But you know I'm never the one to moan.
I fear my health's right up the creek.
I'll have a word with the doc next week.

I'm sorry you have to rush away;
I'd love to pass the time of day,
It's nice to stop and chew the fat:
Bits and bobs and this and that,
But everyone knows what not to do:
Never ask me, "How are you?"

JACK

It's '43 and we're back in UK;
A calm and peaceful July day.
The airfield shimmers in summer heat;
Then a cough and a bang at a thousand feet.
We all look up to see what's wrong,
For we haven't flown the Beau for long.
Jack Beanfield's old, past twenty-six,
And now he's in a pretty fix.
One engine dead, too scared to land,
Control column held in shaking hand.

We're all just coming out of our teens.
Rarin' to go and full of beans,
But Jack's got a wife and kids at home
And has never been a one to roam.
We watch his plane go round and round
And no one makes a single sound,
But we're praying that he'll do everything right,
Will ring his wife again tonight.

Oh please ... don't try to turn that way!
Remember what the textbooks say!
But Jack can't hear: he's terrified,
And no one's there to be his guide.
There's been no time, so much to learn,
So he opens the throttle and steepens the turn.

Please God, don't do that!
Don't be a prat!

The Beaufighter rolls with leisurely grace
And dives straight down with relentless pace.
And Jack, whom many thought a bore,
Is sadly one of us no more.
Though he's our first, he's not the last:

Just another name we knew in the past,
But, for Mrs B, it's another thing
As she waits tonight for the phone to ring.

JAZZ

Come down, David, sweet chariot, swing low;
From what dark depths did such words flow.
The music came from the very soul,
Yet here was the start of rock and roll.
O my Lord...! Their bodies sway ...
The birth of the blues as now we say.
From cotton fields to Cotton Club;
Harlem was the jazz world's hub.
The banjos twang their tinny beat,
Honky-tonk reigns where brothers meet.
Clap yo' hands and stomp yo' feet,
T'was in their blood, old Africa's heat,
But now their cruel masters say
It's to a white God they must pray.
They knew the gods liked them to shout,
They'd find new words to shout about.
Steal away, steal away, voices keen;
Nobody knows the trouble I've seen.
Go down Moses to that deep river.
I hear the sound that makes me shiver.
Ahm standing here at Heaven's gate:
De gospel train am a-com'n late....

Now Louis and Miles can toot their horn,
Ben Webster's sax breathe love forlorn.
Duke Ellington's quite a serious chap
But Thelonius Monk knows how to rap.
Oscar Peterson's a heavyweight;
But for stride piano, it's Basie I rate.
Ella's sweet as blueberry pie

And Billie Holliday makes me cry.
But though I leap and jump about
And drop some names and loudly shout,
I'm afraid that jazz can't ever be
The very breath of life for me,
For I am lacking the essential means ...
The soul of Africa in my genes.

JOCK

Not your typical air crew type,
He smokes a massive Meerschaum pipe.
Balkan Sobranie sent by his Mum,
Tapped in the bowl by a practised thumb.
Far too staid for twenty years old,
Too content for a warrior bold.

He flies his ops like the rest of us;
Does the job and makes no fuss ...
Until one sunny afternoon,
The sighs of relief come far too soon,
For their plane has suffered grievous harm
And they ditch in a sea deceptively calm.

As the stricken aircraft slides below,
What terrors must Macdonald know?
His face stares out but he's held fast
And Jock's a brave man to the last.

JOHNNIE AT 82

She's nearly blind, her heart's not right;
She didn't sleep a wink last night.
Aching back and cramp in her foot;
Her racking pain just wrings my gut.

I'm wakened by her furtive tear,
Though she would try to quiet my fear,
But I'm on edge and I can tell
That she is very far from well,
Though, when the dagger strikes again,
The nitro spray will ease her pain.
Yet I will stay awake with dread,
So restless in our marriage bed.

In early morning's cold clear light,
I touch to see if she's all right.
Happier now that I can say ...
We've not yet reached that fateful day.

KELMSCOTT

Wallpaper will put you on the track
To remind you of this arty quack.
No Nuffield he but, all the same,
How different is his claim to fame.
Tortured springs will loud complain,
Racketing down this narrow lane,
Hoping you will never face
Farmer Giles at arrogant pace.

No chocolate box that I can see,
A dismal place it seems to me.
A turgid river idles by,

Where water meadows dankly lie.
Let's not stand and wonder here
But go in search of better cheer.

A village pub....a welcome sight....
I'm overjoyed....it looks just right.
Mine host will be a lovable rogue,
Jesting in the broadest brogue,
But all I get is a brisk "G'day!"
In a decidedly Antipodean way
And the waitress takes me back in time
To Jo'burg and my youthful prime.

As I stood at the bar, the feeling grew:
Can this be the place that William knew?

KENCOT

There is no way to part the two,
Though that's what natives strive to do.
Broadwell has a graceful spire,
And Kencot's faithful need no choir.
Broadwell has the village pub,
With chilli pepperish sort of grub.
When will it open: that's anyone's guess,
And must we wear our formal dress?
Sadly, the custom to make it fail
Is a man, his dog and a pint of ale.

The larger sort of house abounds.......
Think in terms of a million pounds.
If you need a mortgage, as many do,
Then this is not the place for you.

We're up to date on planning laws.....
Don't dare to build without just cause.

Everything's got to be just right........
In matters of taste, we're always right.
A Cotswold village we claim to be
And our credentials are plain to see.

LITTLE FARINGDON

Now you see it, now you don't ...
Blink an eyelid and you won't.
Lechlade's near but worlds away.
Little more that one can say.
Showbiz glitz has made its mark;
I hear it's lively after dark.
Tradition's got a point to show ...
The churchwarden's still an aristo.

LOG ON

Eureka I shout, the victory's mine ...
At last, I've managed to go on line.
I've entered my password and spelt it right;
I've adjusted my chair to its optimum height.

Now, have I remembered what to do?
Will the browser guide me to Mister Yahoo?
No, I've been invited to ask Mister Jeeves.
What a very strange web my Tiscali weaves!
But, before I can tell him that Jeeves will do fine,
He tells me that I am no longer on line.

I've done everything right, though I don't want to boast,
So why is he such an unwelcoming host?
And, if protocol means that you're always polite,
My reluctant host ain't done me quite right

And look at the harm he seeks to wreak:
He's making me write in yobbospeak.

So Mister Tiscali, you can get lost!
It's One Tel in future at minimum cost.
At a penny a minute, the world is mine.
I'm full of hope and I'm feeling fine.
There's nothing wrong with my intellect
But e-mail comes up with "Cannot connect."

OK, Mister Dell: it's outright war!
I've had enough: I cannot take more.
I think I'll defect to the enemy camp
And go out and buy a first class stamp.

MARCH

It's three o'clock on a dank March day
As I sit here idling my time away.
The window's speckled with relentless rain
And water courses the village lane.
The daffodils bloomed some weeks ago,
Beguiled by springtime's early show;
Now beaten flat, still yellow-bright,
They've given up without a fight.

The trees are bare and no birds sing;
A gloom descends on everything.
Leaden skies loom overhead.
What was it Philip Sidney said?
"The countryside's a healthy grave"
Not so healthy now, my brave,
For I have found there's one small hitch:
Life at eighty's such a bitch!

MARKET TOWN

A school for gals stands in Betjeman's town,
Victorian brick, now mellow'd to brown.
King Alfred stands in the Market Square
Where, once a year, there's a travelling fair,
And cars give way to gaudy stalls
Where coconuts face those wooden balls,
And painted horses go round and round
To a mechanical organ's strident sound.

I could think that time's stood still,
That the mill is working down the hill,
Mrs Martin holds the antiques fort
And fustian trousers can be bought,
The Bear's stone-flagged, a roaring fire,
And countrymen jest in the tongue of the shire,
A noisy parrot at the side of the bar,
All green and blue, too rude by far;
Arberry's selling what a lady needs,
Corsets, stockings and strings of beads.
Not the stuff for urban life
But just the thing for a farmer's wife.
A toot and a hoot that cheekily showed
A train was leaving Wantage Road,
Silver Cross prams and people on bikes:
The sort of town that everyone likes.

But, the following day, the fair has gone
And we can see what time has done.
Traffic non-stop, no bikes to be seen,
A bar-room carpet in tasteful green.
The Bear is posh as posh can be
And full of suits drinking g and t.
The town is ringed by modern estates,
With plastic bay windows and neat little gates,
Where proud owners sport a science degree

And even the occasional PhD.

It's not the place it used to be,
This home of the Oxfordshire bourgeoisie
And it's one of the planners' neat little larks
That, when I first came, it was still in Berks.

MATHEMATICS

I've always liked to work things out,
Find what a problem's all about.
Little boys add two plus three......
Five was the answer that came to me.
As time passed by, I came to ken
That, in modulo five, it seemed like ten.

Pythagoras was the first to arrive,
Made three and four a much quicker five.
In higher bases, the going gets tough
For the fingers alone are not quite enough.
Everyone knows three dots mean `thus`
And minus times minus is always plus,
But root minus one can only get by
By calling itself the letter 'i',
Though modernists have been heard to say
It should be known by the letter `j`.
But "What's in a name?" as the poet said
And my bank insists a minus means red.

If you happen to be of a literary bent,
Then algebra really is quite heaven sent:
Though it's said that statistics are the science of lies,
The facts are there in front of your eyes.
It's just that a stretch, a squeeze or a poke
Can make them confusing for so many folk.

Newton's the man whom I always hold dear
For making Mechanics abundantly clear.
And it all began, or so it's said,
When a Cox's Orange fell down on his head.
In an earlier life, I looped the loop
And towards my feet my blood did droop,
Though I was not the first the first to see
The significance of that letter `g`

MATINS

It's ten to the hour and we're ready to go.
The organ starts up, a chorale we know.
It's setting the scene for peace and calm,
For troubled souls seek healing balm.

"Hi there, Peter, what d'you know!
I've heard a good one, ho, ho, ho!
Morning, Teddy... Wotcha, mate!
It's not like you to be so late!
I say, there's Jilly with her brats,
Howling like two alley cats.
I heard today that Gilts are down;
Tomorrow I'll pop up to town.
Old Stinky Ffawcett gets about;
At Teddy Hall, we shared a scout.
We got quite close, as was the norm,
When I was Radley's head of dorm.
Speak up, old chap, Can't hear a word!
Who's over there with that new bird?

Now there's a liberty, if you please!
That stranger there is on her knees!
A bit too obvious one might say......
Not quite the form in here today!
Let's take a pew, the parson's here.
Bring Bunty round; we'll have a beer."

Venite's come....not all the way;
Jubilate cheers the day
The psalm is said, the lesson read,
The organist nods his weary head.
What's the parson got to say?
My, he's clad in gay array!
He'll spell out what is right and wrong;
We know for sure, he'll take too long!
"God of concrete"....call that a hymn?
We sing with our accustomed vim.

Now the organ starts to roar....
A headlong rush for the open door.
Everyone's gone, the church is still.
It's dwinky-poo at the house on the hill
But way back there,in an empty pew,
Sits a lonely woman whom no one knew

O TANNENBAUM

I think that I shall never see
A thing unlovely as our tree.
It dominates in vicious green
Where a favourite jug was always seen.
All dressed up in tawdry gold,
Silver foil and bits too bold,
Little angels, pretty things,
Bright red balls and tinsel rings.
Twisting wire and fairy lights,
Winking madly through the nights.

I like the holly and mistletoe,
A pagan thing, I'm sure you know.
But now it starts when summer fades
Into autumnal russet shades.
The silver screen shows kids' delights,
Brings worried parents sleepless nights

And it all becomes one jamboree
Which is, by far, too much for me.

I can't deny I like the sight
Of a cheery fire on a winter night,
Carollers singing at my gate,
A yellow lantern, a familiar wait.
Crisp snow around, the fields all white
God's in his Heaven and I'm all right.

Yuletide now is fading fast;
The festive season is finally past.
We've got the problem of you know what:
A carpet of needles marks the spot.
On the Twelfth, my true love says to me:
"Get out your spade and plant our tree"
This is now a familiar tack
So I clasp it tight, trudge round the back.
I'd like to protest, but what's the use
For the garden's a forest of Norwegian spruce.

OLD FRIEND

I've sat in the front of many a plane
But I remember the one that bore my name.
I posed for a snapshot under its wing
And its praises I was eager to sing.
Its engines sang so sweet and true
And served me well where'er I flew.
I eased her gently into land
On metal plates on desert sand.
I thought we two were state of the art
And had no thought that we would part,
But our affair was not to last;
Our time, I fear, was closing fast.
Too soon there came that fateful day

When a sort of debt we had to pay

On a February eve in '44,
At last, our friendship was no more.
We met a most unkindly foe ...
No strain of mercy would he show.
Twisting, turning, dizzily round,
Throttle wide and heart a-pound.
In the end, her body sore,
My dear old friend could take no more.
Imagine how it felt for me,
Floating there in a glassy sea,
To see my friend, all fiery glow,
Slide smoothly down to the depths below!

And then, such quiet ... nothing heard nor seen;
'Twas as if my friend had never been.

ON THE SIDE

A bit on the tall side for a bloke like me;
To peck my cheek, she bends her knee,
But, all too often----and this I hate----
Her lips just brush my balding pate.
Though, just to show the old beast kicks,
I stretch to my almost five feet six,
My white-haired head in perfumed rest,
Asphyxiate in ample breast.

Softly-voiced, a gentle smile;
Surely with no trace of guile.
Could she be my offspring's mate?
For that, I'd have a long, long wait.
The golden band that ties the knot
Doesn't always mean a lot
But, in her dreams, she'd like to be
A sort of kith and kin to me.

A father figure, her lover's dad.....
Would that really be so bad?
But I'm afraid it's not to be;
One thing's very clear to me:
Her fate will be long to abide
Unrequited.... on the side.

OPEN DAY

Everyone's busy mowing the lawn ...
We're preparing for Open Day on the morn.
All the wild flowers that clad our lane
Must wait a while to grow again,
For all the verges are as clinically neat
As any town's suburban street.
No hint of red or green or blue
Has any hope of peeping through.
The gnomes with fishing rods look so sweet:
A pretty picture hard to beat.
The keener gardeners aspire to fame
And label their flowers with a Latin name

Solid citizens toiled all day
To sweep the streets....no thought of pay.
The organist practises what he'll play
Should there be rain to spoil the day.
A plate of earplugs by the door ...
We've had complaints so oft before.
Deaf as a post and over the top ...
Who dares to tell him when to stop?
To a feisty lady it's pointed out:
Don't hang your weekly washing out.
The foolish chap who made that clear
Has acquired a flea in a cauliflower ear.
The village hall's been set for tea
And cakes cut small as small can be.

Laura Ashley for the ladies' frocks
And other ranks must wear their smocks.
We go to bed and look towards
The arrival of the Philistine hordes.

"Come on, old girl, let's be away
And make the best of a summer day.
We're off to find some rustic charm,
All flowery lanes, a little farm,
A village pub to bide awhile,
A portly host with welcome smile.
Yokels sitting on a bench outside,
Girls in jodhpurs out for a ride.
I'll go inside for a pint or two,
Feel at home as I'm wont to do.
I'm a born raconteur when leaning on bars
For I make my living by selling used cars.
My Barbour and brogues were money well spent
For how else would these locals know a real gent.

The air will be filled with the scent of wild flowers,
Tumbling along lanes so different from ours.
We'll hear the buzzing of honeybees,
Fluttering leaves in a gentle breeze.
A village hall where women serve tea,
Huge cakes and scones for a derisory fee.
You can't beat the country for a good day out;
Meet simple folk; put yourself about.

I'll park right here on this new-mown grass
Though I doubt I've left room for others to pass,
But I was here first and I've staked my claim.
You've got to keep well ahead of the game.
So, buck up, Tracey: let's take some pics
Of the rustic life out here in the sticks.
And pick those daffs and fill the boot.
We can't go home without some loot

To remind us of the summer day
When, just the once, we passed this way."

PARTY TIME

It's party time at Number seven
And our idea of executive heaven.
The Close is green and open plan;
On any fence there is a ban.
The Georgian doors are sparkling white,
And Viennese drapes keep out the light.
A double garage is de rigueur:
A Beemer for him and a Volvo for her.
Gervase has satchel and blue-hooped cap,
Molly's lacrosse stick rests in her lap.
The school-run chore we share each day,
Since boarding's more than we can pay,
But we pretend that we're top drawer ...
That's surely not against the law.
We have our pride and pay our way:
Save our pennies for a rainy day.

So down the road at a leisurely gait;
The invite says half seven for eight.
A bowl of punch in the entrance hall;
Hugs and kisses for one and all.
We stand in groups and circulate;
Smoking's now quite out of date.
Wine's poured out, both red and white,
And very soon we'll all be tight,
But the double doors are opened wide
And goodies revealed on show inside.
There's quiche and pies and home-cured ham,
Coleslaw, salads and strawberry jam.
Eating on hoof's a delicate art ...
Glass and fork and savoury tart.

We squat where we can and our glasses rest
On the wine-ringed surface of a polished chest.

Now the furniture's moved away
And we're in the mood to laugh and play.
The hi fi plays a thunderous beat
And shoes are shed from stilettoed feet.
There's a predatory leer from Mrs Brown
And Mrs Jones is going to town.
Mrs Ellis is doing the Twist
And Mister Brown is completely pissed.
Just as well as his other half
Ain't doing things at all by half.
She's asked for a tango and I slink away
For I know of old she won't take nay,
And has been known to sport a rose
And strike a very alarming pose.
Oh no, it surely cannot be!
A hot little hand is clutching me
And everyone laughs and gives a cheer,
Clears the floor and prepares to jeer.

So I accept my fate and give of my best.
Do a Travolta at her behest.
But then my wife totally poops the show
And tells me it's time for us to go.
But when she next goes up to town,
I'll be seeing rather more of Mrs Brown.

PAST IT

Have I reached that point in time
When thoughts must be expressed in rhyme
And I'm forever looking back?
What is it that my days now lack?
I've just been out for a little walk,

Met those new folks, had a talk.
Not too far, of course, you see....
My fluttering heart and dickey knee.

I'm lying back in my swivel chair
And jotting thoughts for you to share.
Purcell's playing on my new hi-fi
And poor old Dido's about to die.
"Remember me!" is her plaintive wail.
How could such music ever fail?
The fading sun is slanting through
Autumnal leaves of russet hue.
It's all so idyllic you might think,
Yet, all the same, my spirits sink.

I want to jump and run about,
Kiss my sweetheart's sulky pout.
In waspish stripes, I pass the ball,
Score the try that beats them all.
Open the throttle, pull back the stick,
Roll into a daring flick,
See the target in that little red dot,
Hold it steady and fire the shot,
Dance to the tango's sexy beat,
So very light on clever feet,
Swim across the lake each day,
Always eager for the fray,
Teach my class the lure of maths,
Lead them through its devious paths,
Share their joy when they do well.
So many stories I could tell.

If it's not a bit too much to ask
And not a seemingly impossible task,
Please sound the clarion, fill the fife,
And give me back my bloody life.

PETER PAN

Sometimes I feel I'm in my teens;
Raring to go and full of beans.
My hipster jeans are painfully tight
And my footwear is Nike and striped in white.
My neck is circled by a chain of gold,
Though this may seem a tad too bold.
Nature has played her very own part,
For my Number One is state of the art.
I drink my lager straight from the can
Like any other macho man
And, to show that I've got a wilder side,
I've bought a Harley and I'm learning to ride.

I went to a disco on Saturday night
And the kids outside all cheered me on sight,
But when I reached the front of the queue,
The face I saw had a menacing hue.
"Push off, grandad ... sling your hook!
Go home to bed .... warm milk and a book!
I think you've got a helluva nerve
And you look to me like a bit of a perv!"

So I slink away and hide my shame.
Macho man has become quite tame.
Then, in the dark, a square of light:
A beacon in this desolate night.
Fairy lights ... bright blues and reds ...
"Party Night for the Silver Threads"
And what a welcome for my aching bones
As I dance around in a jolly Paul Jones,
For the music stops and what do I see
But the girl of my dreams there facing me.

Dressed to kill in the latest gear;
Pouting lips and a cute little rear.

A red leather mini just reaches her hips
And pearly gnashers gleam from her lips.
When she opens her mouth, I know she's from Brum
And she'll opt for a coke with a dollop of rum.
False eyelashes kiss her powdered cheek
And her perfume kills with a powerful reek.
Her dizzy-blonde locks have that Marilyn feel
And, from a distance, they look quite real.
Five feet tall on drop-dead heels,
I know just how my partner feels,
But I'm over the moon and fancy-free,
For, just like me, she's 83.

PLACE NAMES

Where places want to make a hit,
They like to add a little bit.
Near the coast, they feel quite free
To say they're `Something-by-the-Sea`.
If the definite article's far too harsh,
Take your cue from Moreton-in-Marsh.
Middle Wallop if you're feeling posh
But haven't got quite enough of the dosh,
But if you've got on really well,
There's no place better than Upper Swell.
Is that a whiff of a familiar whine ?
"I see your home town's the same as mine."
"How wrong can you be! We're from Cheshire, you see".
O tactless me! That's across the Merseeee ...

I've lived in houses old and new:
In Wallingford, Goring, Pangbourne too.
You'll know where they are, these riverside gems,
For they're all quite close to Reading-on-Thames.

Too much water's being taken out
And rippling streams will dry in drought.
What would those little gift shops say
To Bourton-on-Mud as a name one day?
Now here's a poser for your mind to bend:
Where do the Cotswolds begin and end?
Stow-on-the-Wold is known to be cold
And Burford's High Street proudly old.
They're definitely `in`, I would bravely say,
But where does that leave Kencot today?
Oxfordshire Cotswolds sounds very twee
But more realistic I can be:
I sit in my garden and peace abounds
Till to my ears drift airborne sounds.
So let's be grand, seek a Norman key
And proudly call ourselves Kencot-le-Bruit.

POET MANQUÉ

I can recall that far-off time
When poems I read would always rhyme
And I would try to learn by heart
As tribute to the poet's art.
And, in my own inadequate way,
They're still my model for today.
That "gordian shape of dazzling hue ..."
I take that for my memory's cue ...
For Keats, my long recall is true ...
"----- spotted, golden, green and blue."

I get to grips with metric feet
And my rhyming couplets are so neat.
Maybe I do go on a bit
And overdo the acerbic wit,
But I've met dames avec merci
And torrid words are there to see.

I've known the glancing kiss of death ...
The whisper of his icy breath.
I savour the russet countryside
And reflect on life's fast-ebbing tide.

But, when I take my eager quill
And bend the Muse to my poet's will,
Why, though the rhyme and metre's right,
Where's the magic in what I write?

PUPPY LOVE

It's Valentine's Day ... what's that to me,
For I'm not the lover I used to be!
Though I recall those years ago
When emotions I would freely show
And, even at a raw fifteen,
Cupid's dart proved sharp and mean
And could bring hurt as well as joy,
Even to a callow boy.
Hot, passionate notes passed to and fro
But that's as far as it could go ...
Apart from kisses sticky-sweet ...
Though ne'er our tongues the twain did meet,
For those were passing, innocent days
And ours were not your modern ways.

Girl Guides clad in frocks of blue;
Boy Scouts' shorts a brownish hue.
The Boys' Brigade wore pillbox hats
And did PE on padded mats
And marched about to the beat of a drum;
Were always nice to their dear old mum.
Parties were a frequent treat
At the little houses on our street

And, if we ever tried to shock,
It was by playing Postman's Knock.

We sat in pews at Evensong
And promised God we'd think no wrong.
Yet there was many a sideways look
That gave the lie to our prayer book
And, while the parson gave his talk,
We'd both look forward to our walk,
When we would hold each other tight
And stroll in Sunday's fading light.
Now, my memory's fading fast;
All those faces from the past.
But I remember carefree girls,
With tossing hair and golden curls:
All those long-lost loves of mine
To whom I sent a Valentine.

RAKE'S PROGRESS

What's to love that's not been said,
From questing kiss to marriage bed?
The feverish hands of clumsy boys
Progress to far more sensual ploys
And pretty girls who love to date
Must learn to be discriminate.
I've had my way in fields of hay
With girls who would not say me nay
And there are times that I recall,
My couch a cold and grimy wall,
When, in the dark of moonless night,
I have said a last goodnight,
For he who loves and lights away
Lives to love another day;
To turn another honeyed phrase
And revel in his winning ways.

Young and old were grist to my mill.
I could never have my fill.
Saucy matrons fell to my spell.
A plaintive tale to them I'd tell.
Yet I have a wild and hasty heart.
It's not all practised lover's art.
I lose my head, am carried away,
Cast caution aside and live for the day.
I've floated high on clouds of delight,
Cried myself to sleep at night,
But my flings don't last and I move on.
Where have all those lost loves gone?

Now I am grey, well past my prime;
All passion spent, all lost in time,
But I remember long-gone days
And victims of my fickle ways
And I so wish that I'd been true
Instead of seeking pastures new.
Then I'd not be so all alone
But be a Darby to a Joan.

REMEMBRANCE DAY

It's November 11th and the boring old farts
Are standing about like a load of spare parts.
The brigadier's breast is a glittering array
For he's on parade on his special day.
His topcoat's black, his shoes are bright,
Umbrella rolled and fashionably tight.
Whatever made the wing co. choose
Those awful, tatty brown suede shoes?
What more to expect of that motley crew
Once scruffily dressed in Air Force blue,
Though there were other shades to see:
Perhaps a glimpse of a DFC.

Mrs Fosdyke's clad in Harris tweed;
In the county Red Cross, she takes the lead,
But she was known as "Say Please" Tess
When she was in the ATS
And widely thought to have a yen
To serve the needs of fighting men.

Majors, colonels all abound
But Private Bloggs is not around,
For this is really not the place
For other ranks to show their face.
Not that we're a snobby lot,
That's just a load of tommyrot.

The parson's now turned up at last.
O God Our Help In Ages Past.
The well-known words are bellowed out:
A ragged sort of godly shout.
A limp wrist raised in billowy white,
Assurance that our cause was right.
Those long-lost pals didn't die in vain,
For evil's loss was virtue's gain,
And all those foreign blokes who died
Were clearly not on God's right side.
So into the church good Christian men:
Recite your psalms and sing Amen,
And I'll no longer give a jot
For poor young Fritz, the Kraut I shot.

REUNION

We all turned up the other day;
Invited to the Sixth Form play.
Sat on chairs at the end of the gym
Whilst lissom girls played her and him.
All very odd it seemed to me

And not what I really liked to see.
It was not as if I knew the cast
For my teaching days were in the past,
But I laughed when I was supposed to do
And managed to sit the whole thing through.
Then my eager footsteps quickly led
To a glass or three of Bulgarian red.
Potato crisps and sausage rolls,
Salted peanuts in little round bowls.

All those faces from long ago,
The colleagues that I used to know.
Some were friends and some were not
And some I really liked a lot.
Bitter memories I'd never seek
So I chastely kissed each wrinkled cheek,
For we're no longer in our prime;
Are victims of the march of time.
We talk about our kith and kin,
The situations we've been in;
Painting and bridge and computer skills,
Aches and pains and ills and pills;
Pretending that our lives are full:
Who could ever think us dull?

But I look around and what I see
Is the ghost of the man I used to be,
For I can remember another time
When I was a teacher in my prime
And this was where I plied my trade,
Believed a difference I had made.
The lure of maths I tried to sell,
Vicarious joy when my girls did well ...
But now I stand on alien ground:

It's strangers' faces that abound.
Now there seem to be so few
Of that familiar staff room crew.
My thoughts come round to that dread text:
"I wonder who's going to be the next?"

RUGBY

I started at school in the scrum's front row.
My shirt's number nine I was proud to show.
I swung from the shoulders of ten and eight,
My little legs flailing at frenzied rate.
Both the props were hulking great brutes,
Tiny minds and huge great boots.
A bit on the short side but a fat little boy,
Playing me there was my teacher's ploy.
I played the game as hard as I could
But, as often as not, was face down in the mud.
Wednesdays and Saturdays, I lived for the day;
Especially when we were playing away.
Wigan and Orrell, Widnes and Bury,
To Birkenhead School, we crossed on the ferry.
The only snag to a home ground day
Was cycling home nearly seven miles away.

When I left school, I still loved to play
But number nine was no longer the way
And I was told in a very loud voice,
"Number seven's your only possible choice"
That was the shirt I now claimed as mine,
Though all scrum halves are now number nine.
I used to pass to my number six:
If they did that now, they'd be in a fix,
For number ten is all over the shop....
He'd never do that when he was a prop.

For twenty years, I've played the game
But not all standards are the same.
Thirteen men in a cow-dung pit,
Happily churning about in it.
Often spectators brought their kit
And finished up by using it.
For teams that turned up three men short,
Their services were most eagerly sought.
Then into a communal bath at the back
Where lukewarm water turned to black.
Pint after pint of bitter beer
And those bawdy songs that we held dear.
Yes, I remember that coarse Rugbee
A game for amateurs .... just like me.

SCHOOLDAYS

I've reached an age when there's time to look back
And of vivid memories there's never a lack.
The scholarship won to that Victorian hall.
Where a high IQ was the norm for all.
Mum and dad as proud as can be,
My certificate framed for all to see.
A world of learning opening arms to greet
A starry-eyed boy from a Liverpool street.
New blazer, tie, a blue-striped cap;
Not so easy in a poverty trap.
Black rugby boots, a blue-hooped shirt,
Pockets dug so deep it hurt.
A long, long book-list I had to fill
At the second-hand bookshop on Brownlow Hill.
Latin primer and Paradise Lost
Had to be bought, whatever the cost,
And carried back, for me a treat,
Home on the tram to our cobbled street.

I remember the way school started each day.
Psalm and canticles, we knelt to pray;
Tiers of pews in an octagonal hall,
The sixth form in the gallery as I recall.
The organ pipes spread the length of one wall,
Organist high, on view to all.
On steep-tiered steps, the choir below
Sang descants to hymns I still well know,
For, of that choir, my voice was one
And my love of music has never gone
Since I sang as a treble in Bach's St John

In German lessons, we sat in rows
And sang about a red, red rose.
Roslein, roslein, roslein, rot.
Schubert's music gets my vote.
War had not yet darkened the Rhine
When of Lorelei we sang each line.
Maths was taught by a Double First
But his style of teaching was the worst
For, whilst he surely knew his stuff,
His lessons just weren't fun enough.

"Fanny" Whitehouse was my English man.
He hunched his back, became Caliban.
An imaginary battleaxe he could wield
When he was Henry on the battlefield.
Yet his voice could be sleek as Lamia's skin,
Make sense of Milton's tale of sin.
That I remember him to this day
Speaks more of him than I can say,
And one thing's clear from this memory trip,
There's more to learning than a parchment scrip.

SHILTON

Go West through Carterton's bungaloid sprawl
And, though it's not very far at all,
You'll find a world that stands alone ...
All hollyhocks and honeyed stone.
No bourgeois baskets grace a wall ...
No, that would never do at all.
No garden gnome would dare to nod,
Dozing over his fishing rod.
A Granary lends a rustic touch ...
Was 'Miffy's Barn' a touch too much?
And, when we meet for dwinky poo,
No one's under seventy-two.

We've done our bit in tropic climes
And carried the torch through difficult times.
We know what's right and we'll have our say:
Leaders of men of another day.
Who better then to still the clock,
Regard tradition as our rock
And, where our steps have finally led,
Preserve what's best for the years ahead.

SISTERS

Tracey Flynn was very thin,
Not a trace of a double chin;
Quite unlike her sister Shirl
Who was a chubby little girl.
Shirley was Mum's pride and joy,
But Tracey should have been a boy.
Mum dressed her Shirl in bibs and bows,
All in pink from tip to toes;
Never doubted she could pay,
Bought the best from C and A.

So Shirl grew up to want it all,
Be the belle of any ball.
It's not so easy as all that
When you are very short and fat.

Fortunately, there came the day
When puppy fat had gone away
And Shirley got her hooks in Sid
Who seemed to make the highest bid,
For he was into big cigars
And made his living selling cars.
Engaged, she flashed her ring about,
Though she was two months up the spout.
Two years on, there were two more
And married life became a bore.
Then Shirl began to put on weight
At a rather fast and alarming rate,
And Sid was looking out through bars
For selling dodgy motor cars,
And, to put Shirl's patience to the test,
Mon Repos was repossessed.

But, across the sea in trendy Milan,
Lived a woman who'd been an also-ran.
Poised and elegant, willowy tall,
A super-model who'd got it all.
Now, how did my little tale begin?
With that very same girl called Tracey Flynn.

SUNDAY

At 50 Day Street I was born;
Early, I'm told, on a cold Spring morn.
An iron bed, brass knobs at the head,
A window on the yard, a tumbledown shed
And there, at the end, in our full view,
The whitewashed hut that was our loo.
Whilst at the front, the door brass gleamed;
Doorstep white and pumice-cleaned.

Poor but proud: that's how folk were ...
A breed today that's all too rare.
A kitchen served our every need:
To eat and drink or just to read.
Hot water and bathroom we'd never know.
Our gaslight gave but a feeble glow.
The kitchen range was bright black lead,
By candlelight we went to bed.
Dinner was eaten around mid-day,
The one o'clock gun sounding far away.
Pig's trotters, black puddings. brawn or stew.
That's just what 'scouse' is ... Irish stew.

The parlour was mam's pride and joy,
Forbidden to a little boy.
A gold plush couch of faded hue,
Chaise longue to the likes of such as you.
Used only on Sundays at mam's behest,
When, all dressed up and in our best,
Out we'd go for a formal walk,
Too dressed up to make small talk.
Heads up high; so let's pretend
That we don't need to make and mend.

My words I cannot bear to mince ...
I've hated Sundays ever since.

SUNDAY MORNING

It's our vicar's swan song: he's retiring today.
On Sunday morning, we gather to pray.
The village sparkles on this summer morn
And the grass in the churchyard is neatly shorn.
Cotswold stone, all golden-grey,
Shimmers in the heat of a cloudless day.
The faithful emerge in their Sunday best
From cots they've made their feathered nest,
But of workers' nests there is a dearth
For the meek don't really inherit the Earth.
Everyone here is very couth
And long past that early flush of youth,
But I can't complain for I'm happy to be
Part of this Cotswold coterie.

The parson's Welsh, charismatic too,
And does his thing as Welshmen do.
The ladies think him really fab
And all adore his gift of the gab
For, when it comes to passion felt,
You can't do better than a home-grown Celt.
Blaenwern will remind him of early days
And Hyfrydol is a song of praise.
Cwm Rhondda we'll leave to another day ...
For far too few have come to pray,
And that's a hymn for a male voice choir
But not the likes of Oxfordshire.

It's Parish Eucharist, a rather High name
But it's Holy Communion just the same.
The organist's got a trick up his sleeve
And plays us "Memories" as we leave,
But everything he plays sounds just the same
So it's really fallen a little bit lame.
Now it's off to the manor for dwinky poo,

Red and white and smoked salmon too.
Elegant hosts with a welcoming smile,
Comfortable in this ancient pile.
We stroll in gardens that stretch for miles,
Our wine-flushed faces wreathed in smiles.
What more could one wish of a summer's day
Than a cooling glass of Chardonnay.

As inhibitions seep away,
I'm far too bold in what I say.
Yet there are those who dare to squeeze
When fingers touch and stay to please,
But it's all a jest and life's too short;
For sour-faced critics, I care but nought.
Now is life's autumn and winter's nigh
And, for the nonce, I'm on a high.
So away dull care, enjoy the day ...
As boys and girls, come out and play.

SYLVESTER

Sylvester Smythe was tall and lean:
Half-moon specs and a frosty mien.
He was Head of a very posh school
Where thick was thought to be rather cool
And the first fifteen were splendid chaps
In blue-striped blazers and gold-tasselled caps.
Where Perkins Minor cried a lot
As the cane swished down on his little bare bot,
Although his spirits rose a bit
When Matron dabbed some cream on it.

In many ways so very odd,
Sylvester ruled with an iron rod.
Strong men quailed at his icy stare;
Sins and omissions were all laid bare,

Though a sycophantic few were spared
And arcane secrets darkly shared.

But, though his staff were sorely tried,
Sylvester had another side.
Though he could be a bit of a beast,
Sylvester yearned to be a priest;
Was mesmerised by tinkling bells,
Intoxicated by holy smells;
Loved to sip the holy cup,
Was really into dressing up;
Spent lots of time in rapt retreat,
Pounded Walsingham's pilgrim beat;
Applied himself to the task ahead,
Quite sure of where his calling led.
Not for him the healing balm:
He would be his God's right arm.

Then there came that glorious day
When everyone's cares were cast away:
With glasses raised and spirit blithe,
They said goodbye to the Reverend Smythe.

TALLY-HO

It's a word that's coined from the hunting scene,
Where only the few have ever been,
Where lords and ladies and farming men
Chase a terrified beastie far from its den,
Where Samantha spurs her pony apace
And yearns for some blood upon her face,
To show she's one of the country set
And not just a townie from a summer let.
Outside the inn, there's a stirrup cup
That an obsequious landlord himself serves up,
Whilst stolid yokels gawp in awe
As their betters joke in a loud haw-haw.
The hungry hounds are milling about,
Eager for the huntsman's shout.
The prettiest sight you've ever met,
But you wouldn't want one for a household pet.
Then it's off down the lane at a gentle trot
Till the hounds pick up a scent that's hot.

We know that Reynard will run away
For he really enjoys this sort of play.
It's not at all cruel, Samantha's been taught
For this is the countryman's idea of sport,
And, when poor Reynard can run no more,
And his belly is ripped and a mess of gore,
Sweet little Samantha can have her treat
As she sits up proud in her leather seat,
And everyone laughs and gives a cheer,
For she really is a little dear.

And I remember, many years ago,
When I heard a rousing Tally-Ho.
In echelon port, we wheeled to attack,
But Reynard then could well fight back,
And, yes, I was young and thought it sport,
But at least the fight was fairly fought.

TEENAGER

The streets are glistening, awash with rain,
Each tramline streaming, a long steel drain,
But I'm cosy and dry on a number ten tram
And for cats and dogs I don't give a damn.
This green goddess is my carriage to town
And what care I if the rain's pelting down.
Everyone's smoking, there's a pale blue haze:
The windows all steamed, opaque to our gaze.
Craven A and Kensitas, Woodbines as well,
Abdullahs if you like their peculiar smell.
To impress the girls I like to chase,
I keep my fags in a thin silver case.

My dark blue suit is neatly pressed,
My wavy hair with Brylcreme dressed.
Black patent pumps in a bag on my knee,
With leather soles as thin as can be.
The Grafton Rooms are a temple of dance;
With the vestal virgins I'll take my chance,
For in innocent times, the girls I'll meet
Come only for the dance band's regular beat.
I'll know the ones whom I should ask
By their silver shoes with well-worn clasp
And we shall glide in heavenly bliss;
Not even a thought of a tentative kiss;
For dancing's a test of effortless grace
And Gold Medals here are quite commonplace.

Slow foxtrots and tangos I like the best
And I'll never stop to take a rest.
Sambas and rumbas are grist to the mill
And in Ladies' Choice, I'll never sit still.
Quicksteps require a great deal of floor
But jiving couples are shown to the door.
The last waltz is playing and that's my cue

To beat the inevitable cloakroom queue,
Rescue my shoes, give my quiff a comb,
And walk to the tram for my lone journey home,
For, despite my partners' so-delicate feet,
They're not always the sort I'd like mum to meet,
So, though it was heaven on the sprung maple floor,
It's time for a beeline hotfoot to the door.

TEST PILOT

This is the posting of a young man's dream
For a test pilot always savours the cream,
But one reservation has to be made:
It's a hundred and twenty degrees in the shade,
For this is a place on the Ganges plain
Where to touch bare metal is to risk real pain.

A Spit is started at the runway's end
Or the gauge for the coolant will go round the bend.
The different Marks go on and on
And there's something different about every one.
Before I came, I'd flown a Mark Five
But I go through them all, make each come alive.
The Fourteen, however, is over the top.
So powerful it needs a five-bladed prop
And, if I use full throttle whilst still on the ground,
It won't keep straight, for the torque whips it round.

I've flown a Beau and there are plenty of those
But what's new to me is the night-fighter nose.
The Mosquito is an aircraft beyond compare
And every Mark is waiting there.
I fly fighter, bomber and photo rec.,
All of them made to a different spec.
The P47 is a powerful beast.
I'm a bit put off, to say the least.

The massive great brute stirs latent fears,
With its gills sticking out like an elephant's ears,
But I read Pilot's Notes and leave the ground:
Become its master and throw it around.
After all this excitement, the Hurricane seems tame
But it's sweet as a nut and fun all the same.

This climate's unkind if planes stand for long
And it's our job to check whatever's gone wrong,
So the fabric strips off, a bit after bit,
And I land what looks like a skeleton kit.
Or the wheels stick up, so I fly upside down,
Take the weight off the locks and pump up and down.
Now the oil pressure's dropped and gone off the gauge
And the gyro's gone mad in its round little cage,
The port engine's on fire, I'll feather the prop;
If that airspeed is true, I've come to a stop.
The hood won't open, though I've given it a clout.
Let's just hope today that I don't have to bail out.
I can't call this work: it's far more like play.
I've not had so much fun for many a day.

But, if the truth is really told,
Remembered still, though I am old.
The reek of cordite and the cannons' loud beat,
The little red dot following hands and feet.
Nothing can match the ultimate thrill
As the shells thud home and you make your first kill..

THE ART OF POETRY

I'm lost in a bewildering world of words.
They flutter about like carefree birds.
They're twittering things for me to say.
I poise my pen, then turn away.
If there were one solitary voice
And I weren't totally spoilt for choice,
I could tell a poetic tale
And my clever couplets could never fail.
But poetry's more than just a rhyme.
And words should stand the test of time.
No need for story ... that's quite clear ...
Nor even cries of joy or fear.
So what if tension never mounts,
The music of words is all that counts.
The smoothly sibilant letter `s`
Evoking thoughts of a soft caress.
The harshness of a letter `c`,
A cruel, crude cacophony;
Or perhaps as soft as soft can be,
As Cecilia's music is to me.

The butterfly's crushed with a mighty swipe;
For subtle ploys I'm not the type.
What use the tricks of the poet's trade
If poetry's debt cannot be paid?
And I still seek that hidden part
Where lies the key to the poet's art.

THE CABBIE

Jawaharlal Singh was a very nice man,
A gentleman true from Pakistan;
A PhD, a scholar no less,
Yet modest enough: you'd never guess,
But ask him to come up with Fermat's Key
And the answer would come as quick as can be.
He came over here for a better life
For his three young children and his sari-clad wife.

Now Kevin Pratt was not a nice man,
Though a true-blue English football fan.
Not that he saw very much of the game,
For he was there to jeer and maim.
He hadn't much time for books and stuff
But he'd managed to get Tracey up the duff.
And, though he hadn't got a job,
There were lots of well-heeled mugs to rob.
So Kevin was never short of a bob,
For who would say nay to a muscle-bound yob?

How could lives be so disjoint?
Yet there was still a meeting point.
For Kevin and Tracey got stranded one night
And they rang for a cab in dawn's pale light.
Now you may think it a peculiar thing
That they were both driven home by that nice Doctor
Singh.

THE CHALLENGE

Now here's a challenge made to me.
Why don't you set your poetry free?
No caustic wit, no memories........
Just think in terms of birds and bees.

I walked in my garden yesterday
And a tiny bird came close to play.
A rounded head and an orange breast;
Soft brownish feathers for the rest.
He cocked his head as if to hear
And seemed to know he need not fear.
Sharp-pointed beak and a pulsing throat
And a delicate little trilling note.
A beady eye looked straight at me.
Whatever, I wonder, did he see?
But, though he turned and hopped about,
He never seemed to be in doubt,
For he remained quite close to me
And not at all disposed to flee.
I for one was quite enthralled
Till, in the end, my interest palled
And I wandered to the garden rails:
Four by twos and six inch nails.
I leaned on my arms to view the field:
A sight that always has appealed.
Dozing sheep on the lush, green grass,
A slowly shifting woolly mass.
Yet, in between them, I could see
Those leaping forms, so lithe and free.
For these are the early days of May
And lambing's the order of the day.

So I've no need of my memory bank:
No bygone days have I to thank,
For in my garden I have found

My poetry's new and fertile ground,
And there is more, as I recall,
For, just beyond the dry stone wall,
My neighbour's geese and honey bees
Are yet another thing to please.
The gauntlet's thrown: I've picked it up.
You can't deny my victor's cup.

THE COLONEL

A greying, ordinary sort of chap;
You would not think to doff your cap.
Rather thin, austere of mien,
A bit far back if you know what I mean.
Long retired it's plain to see
But, in his prime, what could he be?
Spectacles perched on beaky nose,
Neatly dressed in formal clothes.
Not the sort to cause distress;
A pedantic type you'd rightly guess.

The manager of a high street bank,
A solicitor of the middle rank.
A classics don in a public school,
Dry as dust but no one's fool.
A circuit judge all clad in red,
Owlish as he nods his head,
A parson of the older sort,
Down on sin and errant thought.
A city gent in pinstriped suit.
Don't let your wilder thoughts bear fruit.

Wait until you hear his voice.
Now you'll make another choice.
A languid drawl that doesn't fit;
You'll never guess the half of it:
A distant style, yet still required:
Lieutenant Colonel (now retired).

THE COUNTRY WAY

This is England at its best;
It's where we've made our little nest.
A narrow, winding village street.
A picture postcard hard to beat.
The colonel rules with iron rod;
He's quite our most important bod.
And everything here remains just fine,
For no one dares to cross the line.
We're told to keep our verges neat.
No garden suburb can compete,
And what raw passions you'd arouse
Should you extend your little house.

Of course, it helps if you conform
And Sunday worship is your norm.
Dress the part in pinstripe best.
Never differ from the rest,
And, when it's time for you to vote,
Pin something blue upon your coat.
Your wife should join the WI,
Your C of E's a wee bit High.
Don't forget the charity round.
Don't even think of just one pound,
And, if you want to have some say.
You yourself will tote a tray.
"Do you ride? Oh, what a shame!"
There, you've lost another game!

Buy a dog ... a Labrador.
Go for broke and buy two more.
Barbour-clad, green wellie-shod,
Now you'll really get the nod.
Put up your name for the surgery run,
Buy yourself a Purdey gun,

And here's a clever little hunch:
Invite the vicar round for lunch.
Dinner parties are a must,
Especially for the upper crust.
Though one thing you must never do.....
Appear to be a parvenu
But, if you are, I'll take a bet:
Your napkin's still a serviette

If you want to keep in step,
Send Toby to a well-known prep.
If Emma seems a shade too tame,
Bunty's quite a good nickname,

Unless, of course, the gals at school
Think Muffin's super duper cool.
Now, just to keep your hopes alive,
Buy yourself a four-wheel drive.
Then you'll turn up the country way
For Radley's annual Open Day.

Try not to seem that tad too bright
Or you will find they'll all take fright,
And, if you are a culture buff,
You'll soon find out they've had enough.
Dinner at one and tea at five.......
Please don't keep your hopes alive.
Burgers, beans and lots of chips?
You're just not listening to my tips!
Your TV set should be quite small.
Don't think of satellite at all.
And, just to show you're really bright,
 Place it almost out of sight.
And. if you still have lingering hopes,
Don't ever watch the TV soaps.

So here's my tale of country ways,
Though that's not how I spend my days.
I live my rural life of ease
And pass my time just as I please.
But I must put my pen to rest.....

It's seven o'clock, so have you guessed?
I've had my tea and, for my treat,
I'm watching Coronation Street.

THE CRITIC

I met a man the other day;
Listened to what he had to say:
"I've read your poems and think they're crap."...
A very literary sort of chap,
For only a most discerning man
Could know my lines would seldom scan.

"I've put things right," he dared to say,
In a homespun, woolly sort of way,
"A word or two more, a word or two less,
An emphasis here, a better stress,
A conjunction to start the fourteenth line,
A better balance that is now all mine."

I stared at him, mouth wide agape,
For my poem now had lost its shape,
So I called him out on the following morn:
Face to face and e-mails drawn,
And wicked thrusts, both sharp and mean,
Appeared upon the silver screen,
For poets are in one accord:
Fine words are mightier than the sword.

Mixed metaphors sliced his writing arm,
A simile struck but did no harm,
Hyperboles thundered over the top,
But I knew how to make him stop ...
Take this, take that, and this and that,
You oxymoronical know-all prat!
My solecisms hit him fair and square

And laid his innermost feelings bare.
The duel lost, he slunk away
For I was the victor on the day.

I waken from my Pyrhhic dream
To nurse my wounded self-esteem.

THE DARKER SIDE OF LOVE

Poetry is a young man's game;
In grizzled age it's not the same.
The blood runs hot at twenty-one
But comes the day when lust is gone;
When Darby moves with grunt and groan,
Though still he loves his wrinkled Joan.

There's more behind than lies ahead.
How long before the first one's dead?
That's a thought to spoil the day:
A dread that will not go away.

Who wants to share such dismal fare?
It's not as if they really care.
They seek to find, in every verse,
Emotions just the same as theirs;
They want to read of passions raw:
Exotic blooms, not withered straw

So I will pen a line or two;
Drift back in time as old men do,
Where every word is real for me,
In the wildness in my memory.

THE HEALER

My mother, a countrywoman born and bred,
Was open and honest, though not well read.
By the hand she took me to a very large tent
For what, I believe, was an annual event.
Hundreds of people were packed in tight;
Sang rousing hymns with all their might.
And, on a platform, wide and long,
He stood and led us all in song.
Pastor Jeffreys looked like us ...
No churchy robes, no ritual fuss,
Yet people flocked to answer his call
And a fevered excitement embraced us all.
The sick and lame were led from their chair
And he stroked each brow and murmured a prayer.
Cast away were crutches, the lame made whole.
How could we believe there was no soul?

In retrospect, it's so easy to jeer
And laugh at those who shed a tear
When loved ones were healed before their eyes
And asked no hows, no wherefores, no whys.
But we're not so naive as they were years ago.
It's psychosomatic we clever clogs know.
They weren't really lame: of that we are sure.
It was all in the mind ... no miracle cure.
But, to simple folk, it was all very real ...
Nothing to reason but only to feel.

You tell of a preacher who did the same thing
And, Christians all, his praises you sing,
And though your faith I no longer can share ...
Would it have been different if I had been there?

THE HI-FI BUFF

I'm mad about hi-fi: I think it's great:
For the latest gadget I can hardly wait.
I know about amps and tuners and things,
Can cut the treble when the fat lady sings.
Auxiliary inputs I have by the score,
Speakers on spikes that are stuck in the floor.
Wow and flutter are of days gone by
For my fidelity is incredibly high.
Acoustic feedback when the basses boom,
Wires festooned about the room.
Dolby A and B and C;
Very confusing ... .but not to me!

I match the impedance and position my chair
For, apart from black boxes, the room is quite bare.
The standing waves ricochet about
And to hear myself speak, I'd have to shout,
For the sound's coming out of every wall,
The woofers so big and the tweeters so small.
I can record the drop of a tiny pin.
The high-pitched crackle of a piece of tin,
Sounds so deep, no one can hear,
Harmonics beyond the human ear.

Everything's bi-wired, the terminals gold;
My gear has no chance of growing old,
But music is something I know little about
And its virtues I have never been known to tout.
An oscilloscope's the way to enjoy hi-fi
And a sine wave's grace can make me cry.
Saint Cecilia's miffed, has slunk away
For twiddling knobs is my forte.

THE HOMECOMING

We'd waited years for that wonderful day....
A council house green miles away.
Fields and trees and morning dew,
Electric light and a bathroom too.
A garden gate, a patch of grass.
Now we had a touch of class.
Empty streets for kids to play,
No petrol fumes to spoil the day,
Although it was a step too far
For folks like us to own a car.

We'd walk to the pictures for a treat
And politely queue for a cheaper seat.
On the wireless, we listened to Music Hall
And Grand Hotel and Henry Hall.
All our dads remembering still
The war they'd fought 'gainst Kaiser Bill.
My dues to my King were yet to be paid
As I marched about with the Boys' Brigade.
Pill box hats and bugle and drum,
Haversacks starched by a loving mum.

Grammar schools for the clever dicks,
And rugby boots and hockey sticks,
Though few aspired to higher rank
Than a job with a pension in Martin's Bank.
Reading, writing and 'rithmetic seen
As enough for the rest who left at fourteen.
What party games young lovers played ...
Postman's Knock and lemonade.
After church, the country walk;
Holding hands and innocent talk.
Then, all of a sudden, the war clouds came
And life was never to be the same.
The boys all went away to fight

And innocence vanished overnight.

Jim and Jack, not Bill, not Ben,
Are back as boys grown into men,
But Jill and Jenny, Emma and Kate
Have chosen our Allies as their mate.
Lovers' Lane is a busy street,
The fields have bloomed in grey concrete.
I look about and it all seems wrong;
Now I feel I don't belong.
Dad's looking old and here's a shock,
They've had to move to a tower block.

My return has brought them joy
But they see me still as their golden boy.
A boy of eighteen is what they see,
Yet I'm a man of twenty-three,
I've seen and done so many things
And now I want to spread my wings.
Though, in my heart, I know I care,
I have changed beyond compare.

So, how do I tell what's clear to see ...
There's nothing here at all for me!

THE HYMN

I told the parson it wouldn't do,
But, "Of course," I said, "It's up to you."
Mind you, I made my point quite clear,
But all to no avail, I fear.
The words may have a trendy ring
But "thees" and "thous", now they're my thing.
The music should have a foxtrot's grace
And glide along at leisurely pace.
Hummity, dummity, keep it quick;
Now that's what gets right on my wick.
"They'll get it wrong, that Kencot lot,"
I ventured as my Parthian shot.
His gentle smile just said it all;
I could have been talking to the wall.

At ten to eleven, I start to play,
Sunday being the fateful day.
The usual din comes from below,
So I've learned to keep the volume low.
I look in my mirror as the tumult dies.
The parson appears and the faithful rise.
A hymn and the canticles - no trouble at all,
But I know we're soon to ride for a fall.

When I needed a neighbour, were you there, were you
there?
When I needed a neighbour, were you there, were you
there?
When I needed a neighbour, were you there, were you
there?
When I needed a neighbour, were you there, were you
there ...?

A lilting melody that is not;
More for running on the spot.

And, for the words, what can I say?
It's never poetry, even today;
So I slow it a little on the first repeat,
To still those jaunty, tapping feet.

Now, who would believe the uproar I'd cause
By making my poor little half-note pause.
 I grind to a halt and make my plea:
"Please sing it the way I want it to be."
We start again and it's just the same.
They're sure that I'm the one to blame,
And they're not going to change their well-trodden ways
For an uppity organist having one of his days.

Then I see in my hymnbook, which I carelessly scan,
"Sing unaccompanied whenever you can."

THE INSOMNIAC

It's half past two and I'm wide awake.
Why can't I sleep, for heaven's sake!
My mind is racing, just won't stop,
Yet I'm so tired my eyelids drop.
What foolish thing did I do today?
It bothers me more than I can say.
Tomorrow there is so much to do
But I cannot seem to think it through.
I sort it out, then change my mind.
Is there a solution I can't find?

Let's start again. Where was I now?
I try to ease my wrinkling brow.
I'm sure I've lost a ten-pound note.
That girl in Sainsbury's gets my vote.
Did I leave the kettle on?
Where's the housekeeping money gone?

I've got an itch in the small of my back.
It's concentration that I lack.
I'm sure that Paul's new pal is gay.
Is Alison in the family way?

Focus my thoughts, let's get things straight.
Was there a question? My mind won't wait.....
Churns around and looks for a key
To what it is that's bothering me,
I toss and turn, get tangled up,
Go down to seek a soothing cup.
Back to bed, I'm wide awake;
Give my pillow a vicious shake
And with frustration I could weep,
For my dearly beloved's still asleep.

THE KNIGHT'S TALE

A gallant knight and a maiden fair ...
Indeed they make a handsome pair,
But, will he, won't he, that's the thing,
Or is this just a knightly thing?
He sits on the fence, a regular toff,
But he'll make sure he won't fall off,
For, rather than meet the fence apace,
He'd consider scratching from the race.
A bon viveur of some repute,
His martial arms a rampant newt.
A warrior who no quarter cedes
To those on whom his ego feeds,
And many of those who meet by chance
Fall victim to his thrusting lance.

But, what about the maid, forsooth,
Who has a passing sweetish tooth?
If I believe what I am told,

Her blood doth course yet far from cold.
Though should our knight fall from his perch,
She'd never leave him in the lurch
But sweep him to her beauteous breast
And put his knightliness to the test,
And then, brave sir, all doubt is past,
For you, at last, the die is cast,
And where, oh where, will you put your trust
When the thrill of the chase has turned to dust?

THE LITTLE WHITE PILL

O little friend, you're tempting me
Asleep in your bed as calm as can be.
Who could believe that your tiny frame
Could make my problems seem so tame?
All clothed in white, you know no shame
And proudly bear your given name.
You're never one to pout or tease
But open your arms to a life of ease,
Where worries seem to drift away
So I can face another day,

But I am weak and can't say no,
Cannot bear to let you go,
And, once I take you to my lips,
I'll not be sate with tiny sips.
I'll want the whole, not part of you,
Like star-cross'd lovers always do.
Then I am lost, for your heart is cold,
And I'm your slave not lover bold;
So I turn my head and look away
To face the trials of the day.

THE LOVER

She's tall and curvy; what a gal!
And everyone thinks she's just my pal,
But there's a secret I daren't tell
For I don't want to break the spell.
I would have to give full voice ...
Admit my doubts yet make my choice.
No longer could I work till late,
For yet another furtive date.
That little thrill of illicit bliss.
Oh yes! That's what I'd really miss.
No carefree drives in my little green car,
Holding hands in a country bar.
Unless, of course, I'm really bold;
Opt for the new and out with the old.
Tie the knot and make the seal;
Ignore the pain that others feel,
Or should I play the waiting game;
Let all tomorrows be the same.
What on earth am I to do?
I know ... I'll have another drink or two.

And, in the bottom of my glass,
It's surprising how my worries pass.
After all, I'm in my prime
And I've got lots and lots of time.
I'll open another; what's it to be?
Rioja's the stuff for chaps like me.
Now, what was I saying; I quite forget?
I cannot get my mind quite set,
But I can feel a rosy glow
That lights the path for me to go.
What's the next one going to be?
The Chablis winks her eye at me.
You cunning vixen, with your pale-lipped pout,
You know you've really sussed me out.

Seductive lover, come to me!
Set my reeling senses free!
Oblivion calls: let's drift away
And, in your arms, I'll end this day.

THE MOUSE

A chimera no less has entered my house,
A vicious beast in the guise of a mouse.
Its defiant squeak is merely a click
But its wilful ways are making me sick.
Left or right or once or twice,
I can't abide these perishing mice.

It's supposed to guide me through the maze
But I've been at it days and days
And now it's driving me up the pole
'Cos it's vanished completely into its hole.

Oh please come out, wherever you are!
Then a sweet little voice calls out from afar.
"Grandad," it says, "can I show you how?"
"I've done my homework so I'll pop up now."

And, all of a sudden, the cunning beast
Is full of contrition, to say the least,
And doing its level best to please,
Like selling its soul for a piece of cheese.

She looks at me with her sweet little smile,
All girlish innocence, no trace of guile.
Now, I'd be able to give it a whirl
If only I too were an eight year old girl.

THE ORGANIST

In Kencot church, the organ roars,
The fleeing faithful storm the doors.
Too loud, they say, quite over the top;
Will it never ever stop?
My feet are stomping with stiffened knees,
My fingers are pounding the ivory keys.
If they can talk at the top of their voice,
I surely have no other choice.

But I am of a forgiving bent
And next time, yes, I will relent.
Abide with Me they do so love;
I think of Ernest and his Dove.
Crimond's old hat but what the hell,
The old ones always go down well.
Sun of my soul to them is dear.
This is what they come to hear.

Ave Verum Corpus too.........
It all churns out like liquid glue.
If simple tunes are not enough,
Let's move on to the heavier stuff.
Handel's Largo.......fare sublime
Ombria My Fooooo.......just one more time!
Berenice's still a sure fire bet,
For you can't go wrong with a minuet.
When it comes to canons, I can't refuse,
And Pachalbel is the one they 'd choose.

Air on the G String......oooh, I say!....
Is one I'm often asked to play
But my counterpoint is far from true
For my left hand doesn't know what to do.
Sheep are sometimes known to graze
But only on my better days.

Of Jesu Joy I'm rather tired
And my style leaves much to be desired.

Though this may seem both bitter and trite,
My Bach, be sure, is worse than my bite.

THE PARISH MAGAZINE

I doubt I could edit a parish mag,
A challenge to a self-styled wag.
My sense of humour is far too bold
And I'd upset both young and old.
My pithy comments wouldn't do
For I can't resist that touch of blue,
But for anything that I didn't like,
I'd tell them all to take a hike,
And, if ever something occasioned doubt,
Like others before me, I'd edit it out.

The parson's words would be very few
For I'd keep him down to a line or two.
For deeper feelings out on show,
The readers know where they can go.
Not that I'd leave him in the lurch
But the place for sermons is in the church.
I'd be on the lookout for topical news,
Solicit my readers' personal views.
But though to read them would be fine,
I'd print just those that agreed with mine.
Our gossip column would be red-hot.
Oh how we'd love to stir the pot,
And, to show that we were quite street-wise,
We'd tell the most outrageous lies.

The WI have a love-in today
But the Over-Eighties cannot play.
Get your tickets from Cynthia Payne ...
Just give her a knock at Rosemary Lane.

If it's raw excitement that you seek,
The vicar's case comes up next week.
We've hired a coach to visit Old Bill ...
Tickets available from The Mill.

Mrs Perkins has a lovely black eye
For cultivating Leylandii..
Mrs Smith next door, to her alarm,
Has been charged with Grievous Bodily Harm.

The Mother's Union has changed its rules...
Membership's free to primary schools
And the local comp will be quite glad
To give time off to a teenage dad

Lord Haughty is eager for me to say
The manor is free for your wedding day
He guarantees you'll have a ball
And a traditional welcome to recall.

I've set my stall for all to see....
The sort of thing that appeals to me,
But you'll not find it hard to see
Why the editor's job is not for me.

THE PATIENT

When I'm feeling rather low,
I know the very place to go.
It's a bit of drag to walk that far;
It's half a mile, so I'll take the car.

The waiting room's full ... that's no surprise ...
They all pretend to be sick in Brize

A snivelling kid is crawling about ...
A single mum's without a doubt.
There's a wrinkled crone with a worried frown;
If I had my way, she'd be put down.
All this waiting's such a drag
And I'm really dying for a fag.

Nick and Fiona: there's a joke.
How did she hook such a smashing bloke?
I hear his voice and I'm up like a shot;
Down the corridor at an eager trot.
I settle down for a cosy chat
But I'd get my kit off quicker than that
If only I thought I could get away
With the things I really want to say.
I start with the twinge in my little toe
But I sense that he doesn't want to know.

I try a rather different tack.
This will get his attention back.
My Herbert's become rather less than keen;
A little bit limp if you know what I mean,
And he wants to buy a bed of his own
Just because I'm seventeen stone.

The dear man's eyes begin to glaze.
I've turned him on with my ardent gaze,
But his outstretched hand is all I see ...
"Goodbye, Mrs Bloggs," he says to me.
So there's the end of my regular treat;

Little enough for a bitch on heat.

But, there's something else I want to say:
I'd not go again if I had to pay.

THE PROBLEM

Now, here's a problem I've set for you,
As ageing teachers tend to do.
A bluff and hearty country gent,
If of a rather portly bent.
A country squire to the tee indeed;
All Hunter wellies and itchy tweed,
Dark, curly locks, and one thing more:
He drives the obligatory four by four.

In another life, I see him still;
Playing each part with consummate skill.
Tattershall check, brown trilby hat,
Beaming smile, a real fat cat.
Leading his winner at the Cheltenham Gold Cup
Or is he the bookie whose takings are up?
An MFH on a big grey mare?
Down with hunting if you dare!!
I sometimes see him play the part
Of a dashing yachtsman on the Dart,
Or ... do I go a step too far? ...
Propping up the Yacht Club bar,
Or the agent for a big estate:
A better tip, if rather late.

Now, who is this I'm taking off?
Can he really be a toff?
Or is he shrewd, a chameleon chap,
Successful wherever he sets his cap?
Or Mister Nice Guy, a warm-hearted bloke,
Truly a paragon for right-minded folk?

Here's the problem I've tried to set:
Where would you care to place your bet?
He's not a knight and seldom frank;
He'd like to help you break the bank
And his three percent might do just that
Before you cross your welcome mat.

THE VICAR

Now is the time for me to preach.
To one and all my arms out-reach.
My golden hair, my Roman nose ...
God's gift to women as everyone knows.
Though I have never been known to bore,
My jokes have been told many times before.
It's just that I can cast a spell:
A classic case of good soft sell.
I gaze about, the ladies sigh:
That one in front is on a high.
We've got a right lot here tonight:
I eye the old bag in the pew on the right.
"Oh Agatha dear, he's smiling at me,
I do believe I'm about to wee!"

Now I'll really wind them up;
Their happiness cup is quite full up.
I'll tell of when I was a lad ...
They like to think me that bit bad.
When I was young, I liked Rugbeee;
I played once or twice for old Swanseee.
My friend liked the game as well, you seee ...
A bold, strapping hooker called Myfanweee.
A bloke at the back gives a great guffaw:
It's one he's never heard before.
The ladies take it as a timely cue

And genteel laughter ripples down the pew.

I don't really mind: it's the thought that counts;
I'll flash them a smile as the tension mounts.
Shall I tell them the tale of that old ca ... mellll ...
That poked his head through the littell nee..dellll ...
They've thrilled to it so many times before,
It's become quite a feature of their folklore.
No, I think they've almost had enough ...
I must be more sparing of the really hot stuff.
My tenor takes wing in Hyfrydol.
I remember it well on the bus to The Gnoll.

A swish of surplice and a smooth sashay
And that's the end of my Sunday.

THE WIDOWER

I rise at six, before dawn's first light,
Though I've slept but little through a long, long night.
I've read some chapters but nothing seemed real,
For my heart has wounds that are slow to heal.
My eyes keep straying to the wardrobe door
And the dresses that once my loved one wore,
And the rows of shoes in a dainty size four
That I can't believe will be worn no more.
I've watched a late film, about what I can't say,
For I was only trying to keep thoughts at bay.
After all these years, it can't be right
That, like a child, I fear the night.
I want her back, yet I dread to see
The vision that might appear to me.

Why does my mind so run amok ?
How long does a mourner stay in shock?
Everyone says time heals one day

And I should do my best to pray,
But time's so slow and I can't wait:
Their God has left me to my fate

Pull yourself up and be a man;
If others can do it, surely you can!
So I wash and dress and face the day,
Eat a simple breakfast, no table to lay.
Keep myself busy, now that's the thing,
Mowing the lawn, doing gardening,
Dead-head the roses, sweep the back,
Put some clippings in a sack,
Clean the windows inside and out,
Try to put myself about.
I must not let my spirits sink
And never, never stop to think,
Try not to recall how it used to be,
Listen for her voice as she laughed with me.

The day is drawing to its close
But I won't surrender to my woes.
I'll heat a pie and then we'll dine,
Open a bottle of our favourite wine
And talk about what I did today
And together laugh our cares away.

But the mood deceives and cannot last;
I live in the present and not the past.
Laughter gives way to hopeless tears
And the night can promise yet many more fears,
So, I'll watch a film .... any will do,
Then maybe read a chapter or two.

I stir as sunlight warms my bed.
Unthinkingly, I turn my head,
Stretch out my hand to stroke her face
But there is just a cold, cold space ...

THE XMAS SPIRIT

These are the days I've come to dread ...
Such dismal thoughts come into my head.
I'm told that this is a festive time,
Though not the theme of this little rhyme.

We've bought a tree with leaves that fall
But my preference would be for none at all.
The same goes for holly, I'd like you to know,
And all that slobbering mistletoe.

While shepherds watched ... oh, give me a break!
How much of this d'you think I can take?
So, when the waits come bothering me,
I see them off with a twenty p.

My kith and kin have come to stay
For that, it seems, is the family way ...
A misleading expression I will wage
For they're well past the bloom of middle age.

Herself won't speak to me again
Until I try to entertain,
Though I don't think it's really fair
When someone sits in my favourite chair,
But I raise my glass for another toast
And try to play the generous host.
The festive days pass slowly by ...
It's not as if I didn't try!

The calendar's cast in the wheelie bin
And my face betrays a tentative grin
"So lovely to have you...come again soon!"
The wife's in tears but I'm over the moon,
And once again I'm on the ball ...
And a Happy New Year to one and all!

TO MY EDITOR

I was born in '23
And grammar was force-fed to me.
The moulding of a subordinate clause,
Commas showing me where to pause,
Adverbs showing the way to go,
Conjunctions making the sentence flow,
Infinitives, gerunds fighting it out
With onomatopoeic shout.
Tenses and cases when in the mood,
Conjugations and all their brood.
Of indirect objects there are enough,
Auxiliary verbs and all that guff.
Ablative absolute for the classically bent,
Evidence of a youth well spent,
A colon here, a comma there,
Parentheses beyond compare,
If hyperbole goes quite over the top,
A little litotes will make it stop,
Improper verbs and common nouns ...
Could that be why my editor frowns?

Iambic pentameters for the poet manqué,
A touch of trochee I dare say,
Assonance, consonance - all the same -
Alliteration's the name of the game.
Fashion now is for poetic prose
But poems like that get up my nose.
Rhyming couplets may well be twee
But are the breath of life to me.
A cunning little foible of mine
Is to match the word to end each line.
Ands and buts I use with care ...
Greedy enough to hog their share.

So, here's the point of my little note ...
pleez dont orlter wot ive rote!

THROUGH A GLASS DARKLY

Supper's over and I've had my fill.
Now Bacchus bends me to his will.
I'll just lie back and dream awhile,
Rid myself of all my guile.
Open and honest as I can be,
Even for the likes of me,
But truth is relative, that I know,
And along that path I'll surely go.
I'm not the one that is to blame
Because I think that life's a game.
Just playing everything fast and loose
And stopping at the point I choose.
I didn't mean to do you harm:
You just fell for my false charm
Though, at the time, I thought it true
When I confessed my all to you;
Pledged my troth and wept a while;
Stroked your cheek and made you smile,
But now our lives are in a mess.
What comes next I cannot guess.
Another glass will make me weep,
Unless, of course, I go to sleep,
To dream of other hearts to break
And other promises I can make.

Bubble, bubble, the bottle chinks.
I'll just put off my forty winks
And get in touch with dear old dad,
Which often happens when I'm sad.
"Hullo Pop! I love you too.
I don't know what I'm going to do"
But Pop is miffed because I'm pissed;
Cares naught for any girl I've kissed
And tries to point that narrow path
Where there's no guilty aftermath.

Yet murmurs words that aim to heal,
But how can he know what I feel!
I'll settle for his kindly ear.
At least from him I've naught to fear.
Put down the phone and raise my glass.
This is how my evenings pass,
But, as I nod, begin to doze,
A random thought gets up my nose!
For, in this so-familiar scene,
I know the man I might have been.

TO MY OPTOMETRIST

If this ode to you is not enough,
I'll try to write some better stuff.
What sort of verse would you like me to write?
Give me inkling, a chink of light.

I fancy you: that's very clear,
But in my mind: that's all, I fear.
Gaze long into my lovestruck eyes;
Don't fob me off with any lies.
Just whisper words I want to hear:
"Does this one make the letters clear?"

The way I feel; it can't be right.
"Does it tilt to left or right?"
Ooh, now I'll really get a rise ...
"I'm going to puff this in your eyes."
O, cruel mistress, witch divine.
"Can you read the bottom line?"
Now I'm yours without a fight:
"I'm going to shine my little light."

Your eyes are limpid pools of brown.
"Now Mr C, look up ... look down."
However much I'd have to pay,
I'd like to come here every day,
To find such joy beyond compare,
Sitting in this leather chair,
If only I could find some ease
From the aching stiffness in my knees.
The spirit's strong but the flesh is weak
And, all too soon, I need a leak.

A dullness besets my ageing bones.
From afar, I hear her dulcet tones.
"Wake up, Mr C. It's time to go."
But of my dreams, she'll never know.

TRAVELS WITH FRED

In Paris, they eat a lot of snails.
One glimpse and then my courage fails,
And there are even nastier dregs
In the form of spindly, froggy legs.

In Shanghai, they see through slanting eyes
And wrinkled old men are said to be wise,
But do you need to go at all,
Just to walk along a wall?

Avoid the Congo if you can,
Especially if you're a missionary man.
They're sure to like you quite a lot,
All nicely stewed in a cooking pot.

Ibiza's an island in the Med
Where the local talent will share your bed;
Where you will party till it hurts

And then receive your true deserts.

Harare's high on the rolling veldt
But don't forget your cartridge belt.
It's no good relying on your natural charm
When the vets come calling on your holiday farm.

If the kids are driving you nuts in the house,
Take them to Orlando for Mickey Mouse,
But, when the black man jumps into your car,
A plucky resistance will not get you far.

The Costa Brava's a favourite place
For cheap red wine and battered plaice.
A holiday scene that's hard to beat
For yobbos who like spewing up in the street.

If pasta and vino are your cup of tea,
Why don't you venture to North Italee.
Florence is arty and Venice is wet;
A Tuscany villa for the classier set.

Though Amsterdam is very flat,
I'm told there's more to it than that,
And, if you're of a certain bent,
It offers joys from Heaven sent.

Thailand's good if you're a bit of a perv.
Enjoy your hobby with open verve,
And, for your sad and lonely life,
You could return with a little brown wife.

Hamburg's the place where the Beatles went;
Then, thousands of squaddies followed the scent,
But, if window shopping is what you like,
Go on fella: get on your bike!

Mablethorpe's plebby and by the North Sea.
I can't say it really appeals to me,
But, if you're the sort for that holiday,
Who am I to say you nay?

In Spain, the Moors came down from the hills:
In Blackpool, old Spooner did jingle the tills
For a week of frolic and that well-known boast:
The best fish and chips on the Lancashire coast.

Reginald's organ; I say, what bliss!
The Ghost Train's dark for a long, gooey kiss.
Sticks of rock and a funny hat.
Saucy postcards where the mums are all fat.
The rifle range where nothing shoots straight.
The B and B where you daren't stay out late.

Dancing on the pier in the afternoon.
The thrills of the evening can't come too soon.
Candy floss and a cuddly toy
Given to you by a gypsy boy.

Cockles and vinegar, a stick of rock.
The Big Dipper's swooping, screaming shock.
Then, back to Rochdale, Bury or Leek
At the end of a fabulous, fairy-tale week.

TYCOON

What's a bloke like me to do
When he wants to bill and coo?
I'm so wedded to my work;
Never known to slack or shirk.
Never dove but ever hawk;
Never time to make small talk.
Hairy-faced and broad of beam;
I'm the one who leads the team.
But I could take a girl to heaven,
Though preferably in a 747.
We'd be happy for a while....
In top hotels, for that's my style,
Where waiters bow and scrape to me
And I know every maitre d'.

But tonight's the night, I know for sure,
When lovelessness will find its cure.
Without a doubt, I will impress.
What happens next's my secret guess.
My mobile peeps; it's from Hong Kong.
Without my guide, they'll get it wrong.
"Buy at 70, nothing more!
What do I employ you for!"
The lady smiles and I can see
She likes what she can see of me.
So, just in case she thinks me shy,
I place my hand upon her thigh.
My mobile peeps; it's from New York.
The export manager wants to talk.
I turn my back on my first date........
"Excuse me, doll; this cannot wait"
"Sell at 80, you ignorant fool!
Do your sums and play it cool!"

Now where on earth can the woman be?

She's surely not deserted me!
My mobile peeps .... I'm back on song.
I'll not stay down for very long.
My spirits get a timely boost,
For I'm in charge....... I rule the roost!

VOCATION

After war's dark years, I made my choice.
For the common man I'd raise my voice.
A land fit for heroes, it was said,
Would be our debt to the glorious dead.
But, if I were to play my part,
Where was I to make a start?
"Give me a child....." the Jesuits said,
So that is where my thoughts now led.
I'd make my bid on the classroom floor
And show the young an open door
Leading to a better life
Where joy would take the place of strife;
Where school would be a magic place
And learning not a rote-learned race.

What cared I for meagre pay
When I could love each working day,
For I could give of my very all
And why should I not too walk tall!
Pupils would respond to my guiding hand,
Love and respect I would command.
Boys and girls would remember me,
Look back to how it used to be,
Never forget that it was I
Who made them pose the question "Why?"
Still questing "If?" or "What?" or "When?"
As children grew to women and men.

I met a woman the other day.
One of my stars, I could confidently say.
I remembered her well from years ago
And all the promise that she could show.
I stopped to chat and collect my due,
As caring teachers like to do.
Cool and elegant, she looked at me.
No warmth at all that I could see.
"I'm sorry," she said, "I can't recall ...
I don't remember you at all.
School was no big deal, you see ...
Especially for the likes of me."

And, with a smile, she turned away
From the crumbling ruins of my day.

WEEKEND

Friday's come and we're all set to go,
Locked everything up, set the thermostat low.
It's late afternoon on a fine summer's day
And we're off for our usual weekend away.
Down the M4 the traffic's vile,
So we hog the centre for mile after mile,
Flash our lights, raise the finger of scorn,
Proclaim the way that others were born;
Especially the reps in their company cars,
Their jackets hung up on neat little bars;
For we're a special breed, you see:
The ones with a second home by the sea.

Bristol comes up and the road divides,
Wales and the West on opposite sides.
We join the M5 with a burst of speed.
It's for the timid to take greater heed,
But, after an exciting near-miss or two,

We're in the middle, having pushed our way through.
I know what I'm doing, my methods don't fail,
But I notice the wife has turned rather pale.
The traffic at last is thinning out
And I have more time for looking about.

The Taunton slip's soon left behind,
But the journey's becoming a bit of a bind.
Thank God for the radios fitted to cars,
Though the local station's all Oohs and Aahs.
I can tell that Exeter's now quite near
When I see a sign point the way to Beer.
The next one says Plymouth and it's open road,
But we turn off for Totnes and our pace is slowed.
It's snail's pace to Dartmouth for we can't get past
The boat towed ahead, with its long, pointed mast,

When we park outside in our usual place,
From a window there peers a full-bearded face.
I try my key but I can't get in
And from inside the house comes a raucous din.
I'm not a fool: I know what's what
And I fear that my house has become a squat;
So we find a guesthouse that's not too bad
And reflect on the joys of a weekend pad.

WILLY WATKINS

Even as a little boy,
Willie liked to smash a toy,
But, to his mum, he was a gem;
The trouble was because of 'them.'
'They' all thought that he was bad
Because he hadn't got a dad.
That was really quite untrue ...
It could be down to one or two.
On second thoughts, it could be more
And maybe more than three or four.
She could try to make ends meet
Like other mums along the street.
The Giros all kept coming in
And she could lead her life of sin
And smoke her daily fifty fags
Like all the other local slags.

Willy knew a lot of men:
Uncles Bill and Bob and Ben,
And Chas and Les and Ted and Ken,
And, in between, there were a few
Whose names he never really knew,
And some he shuddered to recall,
For things he hadn't liked at all.

Willy was a streetwise boy
Whose daily life held little joy
Except when bullying smaller boys,
Spoiling lessons with his noise.
No matter how Miss Johnson tried,
In the end, she always cried.
So Willy's mum was called to school
To meet Miss Johnson, who was cool.
"Willy could do well, you know,
If his standards weren't so low.

He's wild, disruptive and, I'm bound to say,
He makes a misery of my day."

"You stuck-up cow, don't lecture me,
And leave my little Willy be!
You just think that he is bad
Because he hasn't got a dad,
So there's one thing I'm bound to say:
Up yours too, Miss Bloody J!
And here's a present just your due:
This bunch of fives from me to you."

So, though he led them such a dance,
Willy never really stood a chance.

WINE BUFF

When it comes to plonk, I know my stuff,
For the stuff in my cellar is really rough.
I've bought it on forays dear to me,
Across that little strip of sea.
I serve it to friends who think it bliss
But who don't know claret from a pint of piss.
But the label's in French, as they can see,
Pas Appellation Controleeee.
But, when I'm invited out to dine,
I expect the very best of wine.
Mis en bouteille au chateau please
And a different one just for the cheese.

I sniff the bouquet and roll my tongue,
Pull funny faces a tad too long.
Then I close my eyes and give it some thought
For rather longer than polite folk ought,
And, when it's not quite up to scratch,
My hosts will know they've met their match.

I know I'm in for a culture shock
When they uncork a bottle of tepid hock.
Liebfraumilch of any date
I do believe is my pet hate.
The bottle I've brought has been whisked away ...
My little gem of Pouilly Fuisse.
But I have to show my exquisite taste,
Though I know it's all a bit of a waste,
So I sniff and swirl and hold up to the light
And offer faint praise for the appalling white.

The meal progresses, I get into my stride.
Everyone's jolly and my grin grows wide.
I tell my jokes and laugh like a drain,
Refill my glass again and again.
This Valpolicella no longer seems bad
Though I can't remember how much I've had,
And an obscure Venezuelan Chardonnay
Surprisingly takes my breath away.
Yes, of course I'd like another port.
My host has proved a really good sort.
He's not the Philistine I thought him to be
For he sees the connoisseur in me.

So why, when it's clear I know what's what,
Does he whisper I'm a know-all drunken sot?

WRITER'S BLOCK

The pen is poised but the Muse has fled.
So little more that's yet unsaid.
My early life has been exposed,
Though not at all as you supposed.
For many bits have been left out,
Are not for me to write about.
Too late now to put things right
But remembered still in dead of night.
Ecstatic days and torrid nights,
Tender loves and bitter fights.
Long-gone shadows haunting me,
Remembered as they used to be.
And am I too remembered still?
And are those thoughts of good or ill?
Life once lived to the full each day;
Death so often the price to pay.

Childhood proves a useful ploy
To rhyme the musings of a boy.
City ways of the young streetwise,
Little wolf in a baa lamb's guise.
Growing up when times were hard;
Letting no man mark his card.

Years and years in Air Force Blue,
Groomed to the ways of gentlemen true,
Passing the port the right way round,
Tipping my hat when ladies around.
Dressed to kill for the Summer Ball ...
To dance too well wouldn't do at all,
But parties on the married patch
Were quite a different sort of catch,
For we would drink and dance all night
And fly next day in cruel light.

Then years of teaching lissom girls.
Maths with all its twists and curls.
Gals all to the manor born,
My leftist soul in ribbons torn.
Meeting the cream of society,
All so very strange to me.

Moving house and buying cars,
Ploughman's lunch in stone-flagged bars,
Saturdays on the rugby pitch,
Ever there that restless itch,
Seeking change for change's sake,
A thirst for challenge hard to slake.

Now my body's growing old.
Won't always do what it is told.
Aches and pains beset my bones,
And I'm much given to moans and groans.
I listen to Bach and watch the soaps,
Still look ahead; have dreams and hopes,
Do my thing and up yours too!
Remember THE WAR as old men do .
Through a misty veil, I drive the car,
For, to tell the truth, I can't see far.

There's more behind than lies ahead,
Yet there are still more tears to shed,
But, just for now, I'll play it cool,
Fool myself yet play the fool.
And, now I come to think of it,
I'm worth an occasional flash of wit,
So I'll come up with a cunning ruse
And recall that fleeting, fleeing Muse.

WRITER'S CRAMP

I

I've written about my early days ...
City streets and cobbled ways;
Life as it was in the working class;
Release in the exams that I could pass.
Wartime years in Air Force blue,
Daily giving Death his due;
Desert sands and sun-kissed seas,
Khaki shorts and olive trees.
Learning the ropes as I climbed in rank,
Putting my money in the bank.
Golden girls who aimed to please
And not averse to a tender squeeze.
In your face and not so shy,
Sprinting for the winning try.
Pints to sink and songs to sing,
Live for today, oh that's the thing!

II

OK, as a child you had it bad.
You won THE WAR...you're Jack the Lad.
God's gift to women you've always been;
You're the cleverest bloke we've ever seen.
We know you don't believe in God,
You argumentative little sod!
We know that you can pen a rhyme
And get the metre right each time,
So, how about you try to think
And put your memory on the blink
And write about the birds and bees
Or gentle rain and rustling trees.

Hark, I beg, to your suffering wife:
Don't write about your bloody life!"

XMAS WITH NIGEL

Dear Nigel, thanks for inviting me
But you must know it's not for me.
Your table groans with Xmas fare;
Far more than all your guests can share.
The wine flows free without constraint,
Each cork being sniffed for fear of taint,
For, though some wine you're bound to waste,
You are a host of consummate taste.

Eager snouts thrust in the trough;
More bottles opened, cares cast off.
A paper hat and a paper rhyme:
The very breath of Xmas time,
And, afterwards, all those party games ...
Picking out the pop stars' names.
I doubt that I'll be joining in,
No other there my kith and kin.

So, as it is, I'd rather not
And I'll accept an old man's lot ...
Sit by the fire and toast my feet.
A glass of plonk will be my treat.
A fillet steak, some salad too.
I'll drink a toast, my son, to you
And wish you well this Xmas Day;
In my heart, at least, not far away.

1941

We've escaped at last from mummy's arms;
Are at the whims of corporal's charms.
Pyjama trousers we've learnt to wear
Against itchy blue on legs so bare.
We bone our boots and polish our brass,
Look forward to the weekend pass.
That little white flash at the front of our cap
Makes for a special sort of chap.
We sleep on the floor in Regents Park flats
And march round the Zoo in smart little hats.

In Baker Street, there's a Forces canteen.........
Nice, motherly ladies and us just eighteen.
Tea and wads, the old sweats say;
We're learning the lingo as day follows day.
At the National, Dame Myra plays JSB,
Phyllis Sellick at the Cambridge for romantics like me.
A raven-haired girl cuddling close to my side,
To Tchaikovsky's sweet tunes, she was my first guide.
Exciting times, clear now as then,
Boys in a world of fighting men.

A few days more and we're on our way
To the sunny sands of Scarborough bay.
Navigation and Morse and Theory of Flight.
We've just left school so we all get it right.
Then it's off to the docks and a lump in the throat.
We're packed like sardines in the depths of the boat
And sleep in hammocks, fully-dressed in the dark;
Steam slowly through waters infested by shark.

Grey skies give way to dazzling blue....
Fish that fly and dolphins too.
Oversize topees and knee-length shorts,
Durban is to be our choice of ports.
Wide, flower-lined streets, jacaranda trees,
Sun-bronzed girls who aim to please.
The promenade's a glittering blaze of light,
Crickets all shrilling in the starlit night.

The train puffs up through the Thousand Hills,
A thousand miles from Parry's mills.
We all take snaps at Mafeking,
See wild life free and frolicking.

Bulawayo marks the end of the line.
The sky's clear blue and we're all feeling fine.
But, to some folks here, we're a different breed
And not at all the sort they need.
So many of us here with a different view,
A disturbing glut of Air Force blue,
So there's a phrase we're told is rife:
The Blue Plague has come to spoil their life.